Cyber Security Training and Certifications

CERTIFIED

Network Forensic Analysis Manager

EXAM PREP GUIDE

Michael I. Kaplan
(Author)

Robert M. Peterson
(Editor)

01

C)NFAM Certification Exam Vouchers

Vouchers to purchase the C)NFAM certification exam can be secured on the Phase2 Advantage website. Please see the last page of this exam prep guide for additional information and a **10% discount** off the exam fee when taken separately from a class.

COURSE DESCRIPTION

The *Certified Network Forensic Analysis Manager* certification course was originally developed for the U.S. government, and has now been made available to city, county, and state law enforcement agencies. Civilian personnel outside of the law enforcement community are also authorized to attend and will receive practical training for their business environments.

This comprehensive course brings incident response and network forensic core competencies to advanced levels by presenting students with 16 detailed learning objectives. Students will be provided with both experiential knowledge and practical skills that simulate real-world scenarios, investigations, and recovery of evidentiary data in systems and networks. With a specific focus on the centralizing and investigating of logging systems and network devices, students will cover topics such as: Incident Response Management; Live Data Collection; Analysis Methodology; Malware Triage; and, practical lab exercises utilizing the Wireshark packet capturing tool for network investigations.

SUGGESTED READING

Thoroughly revised to cover the latest and most effective tools and techniques, Incident Response & Computer Forensics arms you with the information you need to get your organization out of trouble when data breaches occur. This practical resource covers the entire lifecycle of incident response, including preparation, data collection, data analysis, and remediation. Real-world case studies reveal the methods behind today's most insidious attacks.

Paperback: 624 Pages
Publisher: McGraw-Hill Education
ISBN-10: 0071798686
ISBN-13: 978-0071798686

Wireshark is the world's most popular network analyzer tool with over 1 million downloads per month. As the Founder of Wireshark University, Laura Chappell is undoubtedly one of the best Wireshark instructors around. In this updated book, Laura offers step-by-step instructions on the key functions and features of Wireshark. This book includes 46 step-by-step labs to quickly bring you up to speed with Wireshark regardless of whether you are a newbie or already working with Wireshark.

Paperback: 408 Pages
Publisher: Laura Chappell University
ISBN-10: 1893939758
ISBN-13: 978-1893939752

ABOUT THE COURSE / EXAM AUTHOR

Michael I. Kaplan is the Director of Operations for Phase2 Advantage, a cybersecurity consulting and training company based in Savannah, Georgia.

Michael has written numerous courses and cybersecurity training programs for corporate, academic, and government personnel. He has also developed training programs for Law Enforcement and Fugitive Task Force Investigators on the topics of Criminal Topology, Forensic Document Analysis, and Investigations.

Michael's technical areas of specialization are Incident Handling and Response, Network Forensics, Digital Forensics, and Information Technology Risk Management. He also provides consulting services for government, corporate, and academic organizations both domestically and internationally.

Table of Contents

DOMAIN 01

Introduction to
Network Forensic Investigations

Network Forensics vs. Digital Forensics

Network Forensics	**Digital Forensics**
Volatile / Dynamic Information	Data at Rest
Critical Dependency on Logs	Medium Dependency on Logs
Live Acquisition	Post-Mortem Images
Reactive and Preemptive	Primarily Reactive
External Time Considerations	Internal Time Considerations
Networked Devices	Independent Devices

The last two items presented on this list are the most important and tend to create the most challenges for forensic investigators. In a controlled lab environment investigators may be subjected to imposed deadlines (internal). During a network incident, investigators will be faced with deadlines created and controlled by the actors responsible for the incident (external).

In addition, if a forensic duplicate in a lab environment is damaged, a new image can be utilized. In live networks, damage to one system can have severe consequences to other areas of the network.

What Constitutes an Incident?

While there is not an absolute universally accepted definition of what constitutes and incident, the C)NFAM certification course has found the following definition to be the most comprehensive and accurate:

> *"Any unlawful, unauthorized, or unacceptable action that involves a computer system, cell phone, tablet, and any other electronic device with an operating system, or that operates in a computer network."*

This definition might seem to apply to the discipline of digital forensics as well. However, the focus of this course will be dictated by the last condition of this definition: *"...or that operates in a computer network."* While the disciplines of network and digital

17

forensics share a number of similarities, they also possess very distinct differences in both application and process. Listed below is a side-by-side comparison of the two disciplines of forensics.

What is Incident Response?

Incident Response is a coordinated and structured approach to go from incident detection to incident resolution. Although all of the steps listed below may not be included in every incident – based on severity of the incident and the level of the required response – these steps generally apply to all incidents to some degree.

1. **Confirm the Incident Occurrence**: The ability to quickly confirm or deny an incident has occurred will facilitate rapid detection and potentially lead to swift containment.

2. **Determine the Incident Scope**: It is critical to ascertain the scope of the incident to gauge its level of impact on the network, develop remediation strategies, and ensure no malicious presence remains after remediation actions have been completed.

3. **Prevent an Uncoordinated Response**: An uncoordinated response creates confusion and potentially escalates the negative impact on the network. Proper planning and leadership will reduce confusion while increasing efficiency and effectiveness.

4. **Determine Factual Information**: In the first moments of incident discovery factual information can be lacking and details tend to be incomplete. It is critical to separate fiction from fact and then turn those facts into actionable leads.

5. **Minimize Operational Disruption**: The organization mission must continue despite the occurrence of any type of incident. The control of external messaging, posturing actions to enhance network security, and specific actions determined in advance by the Incident Response Team will all serve to minimize disruption.

6. **Minimize Damage of Compromise**: Once the scope of an incident has been determined and the potential impact and damage has been assessed, any and all actions required to minimize the damage must be carefully considered and then executed as appropriate.

7. **Restore Normal Operations**: The goal of responding to any incident is to restore the organization to a state of normal operation and activity. Contingent upon the severity of the incident and a multitude of considerations, actions to accomplish the restoration will vary greatly.

8. **Manage the Public Perception**: A swift response to managing the messages flowing to the public – and the employees of the effected organization – will minimize the chance of perception superseding any reality relating to the incident.

9. **Allow for Criminal and Civil Actions**: When possible and appropriate, bringing malicious actors responsible for the incidents threatening organizational networks is a goal of both leadership and law enforcement. Following established industry procedures during investigations and documenting "forensically sound" actions will significantly increase the probability of successful prosecution and legal actions.

10. **Educate Organizational Leadership**: Despite best efforts and strong policies, mistakes will happen, and incidents will occur which potentially threaten networks. One of the responsibilities of Incident Response Teams is to educate organizational leadership for the purpose of ensuring past mistakes will not present themselves again in the future.

11. **Enhance the Future Security Posture**: Contrary to popular belief, knowledge is *not* power; *applied* knowledge is power. Educating leadership within an organization does little to prevent further network incidents is no actions are taken to increase the organizations' security posture in the future.

Documentation created by forensic investigators – such as known attack vectors, existing vulnerabilities, and lessons learned following an incident – all serve as the foundation of strategic recommendations provided to senior leadership to enhance the future security posture of the victim organization.

The Incident Response Life Cycle

The incident response life cycle is generally broken down into seven phases. All of the seven phases listed below do not have to be present in each and every incident many will be seen in the majority of occurrences.

1. Preparation and Planning
2. Detection and Identification
3. Incident Containment
4. Eradication of the Compromise
5. Remediation of the Incident
6. Strategic Recommendations
7. Documenting Lessons Learned

Concept of the Attack Life Cycle

Not all seven stages are always part of an attack on a network, but this model can be adapted to fit any incident. Knowing which phase of the attack life cycle is ongoing may help investigators to plan the most effective incident response actions.

1. **Initial Compromise**: The initial compromise is accomplished by bypassing perimeter defenses and accessing the network through a targeted weakness or user account. During this first phase, a malicious actor will compromise one or more systems using a variety of tactics such as social engineering or exploiting a known technical vulnerability.

The attacker can then successfully execute malicious code on the victims' system. The most common attack vectors for an initial compromise tend to be Internet-facing systems and/or third-party applications.

2. **Establish a Foothold**: Once attackers successfully execute the initial compromise, they need to ensure they are able to maintain remote access to that system. This can be done by a variety of methods such as the installation of persistent backdoors, the execution of additional binaries and/or shellcode, or by the compromise of legitimate user credentials.

   In the majority of cases, the attacker will also take this opportunity to establish a "command and control" (C2) relationship between the victims' system and their own, allowing instructions and information to be transferred between the attacker and victim systems as needed.

3. **Escalate Privileges**: Once attackers successfully establish a foothold in the victims' system, their next mission is to escalate their level of privilege within the network. The higher the level of privilege an attacker can gain within a network, the greater the access to systems and data become available.

   Using malicious code, the attacker can command the victims' system to dump password hashes and tokens, which can then be subjected to password cracking software at the attackers' leisure offline. Other malicious scripts can facilitate keystroke and credential logging, allowing the attacker to capture legitimate user credentials and compromise additional accounts.

4. **Conduct Internal Reconnaissance**: Once an attacker has escalated privileges and has gained access to various accounts at various levels of privilege, the next phase in the process is conducting internal reconnaissance. The attackers' goal is to learn as much as possible about the users, data, and systems in the network.

It is as this stage attackers with the highest degree of expertise spend the majority of their time and effort. As the attackers explore the victims' environment they will typically focus on the following key objectives:

    a. Enumeration of the network topology to become familiar with the physical and logical addresses of network devices including IDS/IPS, routers, switches, firewalls, servers, and information flows.

    b. Identify critical systems and data such as database servers containing financial or personally identifiable information belonging to the organizations' clients and partners.

    c. Identify key users within the network including their roles, responsibilities, and level of privilege. In larger networks with hundreds of thousands of users, the ability to identify a small group of users with the highest level of privileges makes the attackers' mission much easier.

    d. Identify information flows within the network to understand how information typically travels between systems. The attacker can use this data to develop a blending methodology and mask the way they transfer data in and out of the network.

5. **Move Laterally**: Once the attacker has successful conducted an internal reconnaissance and is generally familiar with the network, an attempt will be made to move laterally between systems of interest.

Common methods of lateral movement within systems and networks includes accessing network share functionality, compromising and corrupting the Windows Task Scheduler to automate the execution of malicious code, co-opting remote desktop computer to send and receive data as needed, and taking advantage of virtual networking computing technologies to mask and conceal lateral movement throughout the network.

6. **Maintain a Presence**: Once an attacker has successfully executed a lateral movement strategy and has access to multiple systems within a network, it is necessary for them to be able to maintain their presence – preferably without detection.

   To ensure this continued access, attackers will typically install multiple families of backdoors (with different signatures), identify and comprise backdoors to legitimate applications (for upgrading and maintenance), and access additional Virtual Private Networks (VPN's) to conceal their presence as they traverse the network.

7. **Complete the Mission**: Malicious actors who compromise systems and networks typically do so with a particular goal in mind: theft of funds or data, modification of system information, blackmail and/or extortion, and numerous other motivations known only to them.

   Once the attacker accomplish their goal, they have technically "completed the mission." If they have remained undiscovered, the mission does not typically end with accomplishing the first goal.

   An attacker will usually attempt to maintain an active presence in the system, and it is not unusual to see the attack life cycle repeated frequently over time. Attackers may also choose to sell detailed network topologies to other malicious actors which, in turn, utilize different tools and tactics to accomplish different goals.

[This page intentionally left blank]

DOMAIN 01

Introduction to Network Forensic Investigations

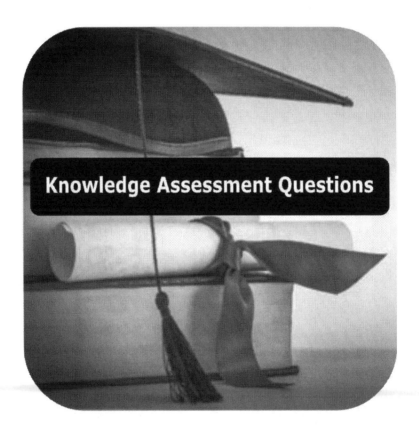

The following knowledge assessment questions are presented in true / false, multiple choice, and fill-in-the-blank formats. The correct answers are provided in an Answer Key at the end of this text. These questions may or may not be presented on the actual certification exam.

Domain 01: Knowledge Assessment Questions

Incident Response is a _____ and structured approach to go from incident detection to resolution.

A. Professional

B. Factual

C. Coordinated

D. Limited

E. None of the Above

Which of the following characteristics is **not** a discipline of network forensic investigations?

A. Volatile and/or Dynamic Information

B. Critical Dependency on Logs

C. Reactive and Preemptive

D. Internal Time Considerations

E. All of the Above

The first stage in the seven stages of the Attack Life Cycle Model is _____.

A. Escalate Privileges

B. Initial Compromise

C. Maintain a Presence

D. Conduct Interviews

E. None of the Above

Which of the following statements does not apply to the Initial Compromise phase of the attack life cycle model?

A. Social Engineering

B. Successfully Execute Malicious Code

C. Install a Persistent Backdoor

D. Exploiting a Vulnerability

E. All of the Above

Domain 01: *Introduction to Network Forensic Investigations*

When an attacker first attempts to compromise a victim's system, one of the least likely methods to be employed with be to _____.

A. Exploit a Hardware Vulnerability

B. Exploit a Software Vulnerability

C. Access a Server Console

D. Social Engineering

E. None of the Above

Which of the following statements applies to the Escalate Privileges phase of the attack life cycle model?

A. Greater Access to Systems and/or Data

B. Compromising Multiple Accounts

C. Password Hash and/or Token Dumping

D. Password Cracking

E. All of the Above

When an attacker conducts internal reconnaissance within a compromised network, the goal of that effort is to _____.

A. Enumerate the Network Topology

B. Determine User Responsibilities

C. Identify Critical Systems

D. Understand Key Roles

E. All of the Above

Which of the following statements does **not** apply to the Internal Reconnaissance phase of the attack life cycle model?

A. Workflow Reporting

B. Enumerate the Network Topology

C. Key Roles and Responsibilities

D. Explore the Victim Environment

E. All of the Above

Domain 01: *Introduction to Network Forensic Investigations*

The second stage in the seven stages of the Attack Life Cycle Model is _____.

A. Establish a Foothold

B. Internal Reconnaissance

C. Malware Triage

D. Life Acquisition

E. None of the Above

Which of the following statements applies to the Establish Foothold phase of the attack life cycle model?

A. Keystroke and/or Credential Logging

B. Establish C2 with the Victim System

C. Password Hash and/or Token Dumping

D. Password Cracking

E. All of the Above

Definition of Incident: "*Any unlawful, _____, or unacceptable action that involves a computer system, cell phone, tablet, and any other electronic device with an operating system, or that operates in a computer network.*"

A. Undefined

B. Unknown

C. Unauthorized

D. Uncategorized

E. All of the Above

The seventh step taken by an investigator conducting an Incident Response is _____.

A. Tag and Secure Evidence

B. Document Lessons Learned

C. Write a Final Report

D. Confirm the Remediation

E. None of the Above

Domain 01: *Introduction to Network Forensic Investigations*

Incident Response is an informal and flexible approach to go from incident detection to resolution.

1. True
2. False

Digital forensics focuses on independent devices and is primarily preemptive, while network forensics focuses on networked devices and is primarily reactive.

1. True
2. False

In the discipline of network forensics, internal time considerations drive and shape the investigators' live acquisition strategies.

1. True
2. False

The field of digital forensics typically has a moderate dependency on log files, while network forensics typically relies on a critical dependency on log files.

1. True
2. False

Not all seven stages are always part of the attack life cycle, but this model can be adapted to fit any incident.

1. True
2. False

The discipline of Network Forensics focuses on data at rest on post-mortem images located on independent devices.

1. True
2. False

DOMAIN 02

Overview of
Common Network Devices

A Critical Dependency on Logs

Whereas digital forensics (aka *dead box*) depends heavily on memory to generate evidence and timelines, network forensics (aka *live acquisition*) has a critical dependency on logs to achieve the same objectives. Although memory forensics does have a role to play, volatile memory tends to recycle quickly in a network.

For example, *prefetch* and *shim cache* functionality may yield crucial evidence on an individuals' personal computer. However, in a large network with a high churn rate, the limited number of entries retained in each (128 and 1,024, respectively) may only last for seconds before being overwritten.

Logs are composed of log entries; each entry contains information related to a specific event that has occurred within a system or network. All network devices have a logging functionality and their logs can be retained for much longer periods of time. The length of time logs are retained is contingent upon the device's settings, criticality within the network, and the needs of the organization the network is serving.

Firewalls

A *firewall* is a security monitoring device that controls incoming and outgoing network traffic based on predetermined security rules. They are used to establish barriers between trusted (internal) and untrusted (public) segments of the network and between trusted (internal) segments as well.

All firewalls, whether physical (hardware) or virtual (software) operate on a rule-based configuration based on security needs established by the organization. Listed below are three types of firewalls investigators will typically encounter in larger networks.

1. Network-Based Firewalls
2. Host-Based Firewalls
3. Application Layer Firewalls

Each type of firewall listed will be discussed in greater detail in the following sections.

Domain 02: *Overview of Common Network Devices*

General Functionality of Firewalls

Firewalls will typically only allow data packets which pass specific security criteria (rules) to enter or leave a network or a segment of a network. An overview of general firewall functionality is listed below.

1. Packet Inspection
2. Permit Traffic
3. Deny Traffic
4. Encrypt Traffic
5. Decrypt Traffic
6. Proxy Traffic

Content Filtering

Content filtering is blocking data based on its content, rather than its source, and is commonly used to filter email and website access. Listed below are common criteria administrators utilize to create content filtering rules.

1. Attachments   (Such as .EXE Files)
2. Email Headers
3. Language Rules
4. Specific Phrases
5. Blacklisted URL's
6. Bayesian Inference   (Probability Algorithm for Spam)

Stateless Firewall Inspection

Stateless firewalls use input from the data source, destination address, and other key values to assess whether network traffic will be allowed. The decision to allow or deny traffic is based on *static information* – unchanging rules programmed into the firewall. Stateless firewalls deliver fast inspection performance and work effectively in high-traffic networks.

The trade-off for performance is they can only inspect individual data packets in isolation without the ability to discern the relationship between the inspected traffic in the stream. As a result, they cannot detect more advanced multipacket threats. They are primarily used in residential settings as this limitation makes them unsuitable to secure large commercial networks.

Stateful Firewall Inspection

A *stateful firewall* uses configured rules to monitor the state of network connections such as TCP streams, UDP datagrams, and ICMP messages. Also known as dynamic packet filtering, these devices determine access based multiple factors associated with the connection itself. Listed below are primary factors to consider when determining whether access to the network will be granted.

1. Monitors the State of all Connections
2. Monitors the Validity of all Connections
3. Monitors the Context of all Connections

Stateful devices allow for customizable rules which does provide advantages but creates a higher degree of latency in the process. The higher degree of latency – in combination with customizable rules – make it difficult to manage Access Control Lists (ACL's) at larger scales.

Network-Based Firewalls

Network-based firewalls are security devices used to stop or mitigate unauthorized access to private networks connected to the Internet. They are usually placed at the network edge to separate internal and external devices, and to protect Large Area Networks (LAN's) from the public Internet.

The firewall ports are connected to switches that direct traffic using OSI Layer 3 and 4 access rules. Proper configuration of these devices is a critical factor which requires a significant degree of skill. As a result, network-based firewalls are typically used in enterprise networks.

Host-Based Firewalls

A *host-based firewall* is a piece of software running on a single host that can restrict incoming and outgoing network activity for that host only. Since it is confined to the host it is not protected by any additional network security.

Host-based firewalls are usually configured to *deny by default*; if a rule is not created to allow specific traffic access will be denied. Rules and permissions can be based on access lists or applications. These firewalls also monitor inbound email, outbound email, and offer malware prevention capabilities. Because the firewalls are not centrally managed they can be difficult to manage at larger scales.

Application Layer Firewalls

Application layer firewalls, also known as *Web Application Firewalls* (WAF) use a series of rulesets to determine whether to block or allow communications to or from specified applications. These firewalls are designed to monitor and control the execution of applications and their associated files.

Application layer firewalls can operate in passive or active modes. In *passive mode*, the device will monitor and report on traffic but will not interfere with its ability to interact with the network. In active mode, it will monitor and inspect traffic and decide to allow or deny access to the network based on its rulesets.

The ability to update and patch these devices remotely from a central location makes them much easier to manage at larger scales than host-based firewalls.

Firewall Log Information

Firewall logs not only help to isolate compromises and incidents, but they can also help to specify the normal operations and baselines of the device. Listed below are several examples of the information contained within firewall logs and associated reporting.

1. Rejected Authentication Attempts

2. Firewall Configuration Modifications
3. Dropped and/or Rejected Traffic
4. The Granting of Administrator Access
5. Identifying Port Scans and Sweeps
6. All Security and Threat Alerts Generated
7. URL and Traffic Filtering Reports

Network Switches

A *network switch* is a device that connects other network devices and manages the flow of data by directing and sending packets to the intended recipient. They allow network devices to communicate with each other and route network traffic based on packet destination data.

Investigators will encounter two types of switches in enterprise environments: *unmanaged* and *managed*. Unmanaged switches have no configuration capabilities – they are "plug and play" out of the box. Managed switches can be configured using rulesets which make them a better option from a security perspective. Both types of switches operate at the OSI Layer 2 (Data Link) level.

Although network switches lack the advanced capability of routers they still provide an efficient method for allowing communication between devices without data collisions.

Network Switch Log Information

Network switches generate valuable log information about network traffic, accepted and/or rejected traffic, predefined reports, and security alerts. Listed below are several examples of useful information contained within network switch logs.

1. Logon Attempts
2. Configuration and Modifications
3. System Events
4. Switch Connections
5. Traffic Reports by Protocol

Network Routers

A *network router* inspects a data packets' destination address, calculates the best way for it to reach its destination, and then forwards it accordingly. Routers are typically stand-alone components in a network whether they are used as physical (hardware) or virtual (software) devices.

Investigators will encounter two types of routers in enterprise networks: *static* and *dynamic*. *Static routers* are manually configured and use only the programmed rulesets to make access decisions. *Dynamic routers* are configured to make access decisions based on the activity in a network. Both types of routers can also perform Network Address Translation (NAT) and make access decisions based on routing tables.

Access Control Lists (ACL's)

An *access control list* (ACL) provides rules that are applied to port numbers or IP addresses, each with hosts and/or networks permitted to use the service. ACL's are designed to control the flow of network traffic and restrict unnecessary traffic for better performance.

Access control lists also specify access rules for network security purposes. Listed below are the three primary functions ACL's provide in an enterprise network environment.

1. Determine Sever, Network, and Services Access
2. Monitoring of Ingress and Egress Traffic
3. Monitoring of Internal Traffic Flows

Intrusion Detection Systems (IDS)

Intrusion Detection Systems (IDS) contain several components including sensors, a configuration and monitoring console, and a database to record events. They perform their security function utilizing two different methods of detection: *misuse detection* and *anomaly detection*.

Misuse detection is based on signatures (rulesets) much like those of devices previously described in this section. *Anomaly detection* is based on activity, or patterns of activities, observed and logged during interaction with the network environment.

The logging of network activity and generation of security notifications and alerts are the two capabilities which provide the greatest benefit to investigators. Listed below are several examples of log information which may provide crucial information during investigations.

1. Network Configuration Changes   (Ports)
2. Session Termination   (Malicious Traffic)
3. Deceptive Re-Routing   (Honeypots)

Intrusion Prevention Systems (IPS)

An *Intrusion Prevention System* (IPS) is a security / threat prevention technology that analyzes network traffic and takes automated actions when needed. An IPS selectively logs on actions taken – not all network activity – which serves to reduce overall security incidents while simultaneously enhancing privacy protection and enforcement.

By utilizing reputation-based management of URL's and the evaluation of anomalous network behaviors (potential threats) the IPS is capable of providing multiple levels of protection.

Additionally, an IPS is capable of *dynamic threat response*, a series of automated defensive actions that do not require human intervention in order to be initiated.

IDS / IPS Log Information

Network architectures are never identical and setting up rules to filter the vast amount of security logs generated is both important and time consuming. However, it is well worth the effort when it is time for investigators to review the logging information generated from these systems.

Listed below are several examples of the types of data that can be gathered from IDS / IPS logs.

1. Malware Attacks
2. Exported Data and Files
3. Unauthorized Port Scans
4. Errors on Network Devices
5. Anomalous Information Flows
6. Security Alerts and Responses
7. Unexpected Processes and Services

Unified Threat Management (UTM)

Unified threat management is an approach in which a single hardware or software installation provides multiple security functions for the network. Listed below are several capabilities and functionalities offered by UTM devices.

1. Network Firewall and Packet Inspection
2. Network IDS / IPS (or NIDS / NIPS)
3. Gateway Anti-Virus Capability
4. Web Proxy and Content Filtering
5. Data Loss Prevention
6. Virtual Private Network Capability
7. SIEM Implementation and Reporting

Unified Threat Management: Advantages

A Unified Threat Management device may look like a traditional hardware firewall but is an efficient security tool that combines multiple systems into a single platform.

There are many advantages associated with utilizing UTM devices which makes them attractive to administrators lacking the time and/or staff to monitor and maintain multiple devices placed within a large enterprise network environment.

Listed below are several advantages provided by UTM devices that make them an attractive option to both network administrators and investigators.

1. Simplified Installation and Maintenance
2. Simplified Configuration and Management
3. Equipment and Payroll Cost Savings
4. Reduced Number of Software Licenses
5. Avoids Redundancy of Capabilities
6. Device Transparency Enhances Security

Unified Threat Management: Disadvantages

As robust as Unified Threat Management devices sound, and as important a role as they play in providing security to networks, there are several weaknesses that can be exploited. Listed below are several disadvantages associated with UTM devices that should be considered prior to their use in a network environment.

1. **Presents a Single Point of Failure**: When a large network containing multiple security devices in a network environment experience the failure of a single device, that device can be removed while other devices continue to perform their security function. When all network security features reside within one device – and that devices fails – the network has lost all of its security capability.

2. **Limited Availability of Updates**: Vendors regularly publish update for their security devices. In a large network containing devices from multiple vendors, updates and patches will always be available at different times. Unified Threat Management vendors tend to be slower to release updates because of the complexity of their devices and the variety of services they perform.

3. **No Specialization Limits Implementation**: Security devices such as IDS / IPS can be configured to perform many functions within multiple segments of an enterprise network. A UTM device by its nature is not specialized, a factor that limits its implementation within the network.

4. **Susceptible to Overloads and Crashes**: Unified Threat Management devices are designed such that one device can perform the functions of many devices. The increased workload and lack of redundancy (delegating tasks to other security devices) makes it susceptible to overloads and crashes.

5. **Less Granular Rules and Settings**: Unified Threat Management devices – because of their lack of ability to specialize – tend to be less capable of allowing network administrators to program granular rules and settings. The more granular a ruleset is made for a device the better protection it can provide the network.

6. **One Appliance Facilitates Vendor Lock-In**: In a large enterprise network investigators will usually encounter a variety of security devices supported by different vendors. If for any reason a vendor falls short of its obligations and cannot provide the expected level of support needed, the organization can discontinue use of that vendor (and their devices) procure services from another provider.

   That level of flexibility does not exist when dealing with a Unified Threat Management vendor that provides for the security needs of an organization – in a single appliance. The ability of using one vendor as a bargaining tool with other vendors has been removed as well.

DOMAIN 02

Overview of
Common Network Devices

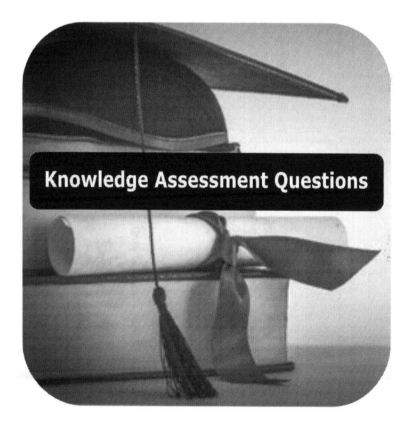

The following knowledge assessment questions are presented in true / false, multiple choice, and fill-in-the-blank formats. The correct answers are provided in an Answer Key at the end of this text. These questions may or may not be presented on the actual certification exam.

Domain 02: Knowledge Assessment Questions

_____ will typically only allow data packets which pass specific security criteria (rules) to enter or leave a network or a segment of a network.

A. Firewalls

B. Switches

C. Routers

D. Bridges

E. None of the Above

Which of the choices listed below is considered to be an advantage of a Unified Threat Management device?

A. Less Granular Rules and Settings

B. Limited Availability of Updates

C. One Appliance Facilitates Vendor Lock-In

D. Avoids Redundancy of Capabilities

E. None of the Above

A _____ may look like a traditional hardware firewall but is an efficient security tool that combines multiple systems into a single platform.

A. Network Switch

B. UTM Device

C. Host-Based Firewall

D. Access Control List

E. None of the Above

Which of the choices listed below is considered to be a characteristic or function of a firewall?

A. Allows Network Devices to Communicate

B. Performs Network Address Translation

C. Operates on a Rule-Based Configuration

D. Designed to Control the Flow of Traffic

E. None of the Above

A _____ uses configured rules to monitor the state of network connections such as TCP streams, UDP datagrams, and ICMP messages.

A. Stateless Firewall

B. Network Switch

C. Stateful Firewall

D. Network Router

E. None of the Above

Which of the choices listed below is considered to be a characteristic or function of an Intrusion Protection System (IPS)?

A. Traffic Restriction for Better Performance

B. Evaluates Anomalous Behaviors of Threats

C. Decisions are Based on Routing Tables

D. Routing Based on Packet Destination Data

E. None of the Above

A _____ inspects a data packets' destination address, calculates the best way for it to reach its destination, and then forwards it accordingly.

A. Network Switch

B. Host-Based Firewall

C. Network-Based Firewall

D. Network Router

E. None of the Above

Which of the choices listed below is considered to be a characteristic or function of stateful firewall inspection?

A. Inspects Individual Packets in Isolation

B. Primarily Used in Commercial Settings

C. Decisions are Based on Dynamic Information

D. Not Effective in High-Traffic Networks

E. None of the Above

Domain 02: *Overview of Common Network Devices*

A(n) _____ is a piece of software running on a single host that can restrict incoming and outgoing network activity for that host only.
A. Host-Based Firewall
B. Application Layer Firewall
C. Network-Based Firewall
D. Network Switch
E. None of the Above

Which of the choices listed below is a report an investigator would expect to find when reviewing IDS / IPS log information?
A. Standard Information Flows
B. Expected Processes and Services
C. Authorized Port Scans
D. Errors on Network Devices
E. None of the Above

A(n) _____ provides rules that are applied to port numbers or IP addresses, each with hosts and/or networks permitted to use the service.
A. Stateful Firewall
B. Access Control List
C. Intrusion Detection System
D. Stateless Firewall
E. None of the Above

Which of the choices listed below is considered to be a characteristic or function of an unmanaged network switch?
A. Routing Based on Packet Origination Data
B. Operates at OSI Layer 3 (Network Layer)
C. Allows Communication without Collisions
D. Customizable Configuration Options
E. None of the Above

A router is a security monitoring device that controls incoming and outgoing network traffic based on predetermined security rules.

1. True

2. False

As robust as UTM's sound and as important a role as they play in providing security to networks, there are several weaknesses that can be exploited.

1. True

2. False

Network switches use input from the data source, destination address, and other key values to assess whether network traffic will be allowed.

1. True

2. False

An Intrusion Prevention System is a security / threat prevention technology that analyzes network traffic and takes automated actions when needed.

1. True

2. False

A host-based firewall is a device that connects other network devices and manages the flow of data by directing and sending packets to the intended recipient.

1. True

2. False

An access control list provides rules that are applied to port numbers or IP addresses, each with hosts and/or networks permitted to use the service.

1. True

2. False

DOMAIN 03

Overview of
Common Network Services

Enterprise Services Overview

Every enterprise network has a support infrastructure that provides key services necessary to operate and conduct business. While the topologies may differ the devices remain constant, and many of the devices useful to network investigators are not security related. Listed below are standard functionalities used to support the daily operations of enterprise networks.

1. Network Infrastructure
2. Enterprise Management
3. Antivirus, NIDS, and NIPS
4. Application Support
5. Servers (Web, DNS, Database)

Enterprise DHCP

Most enterprises utilize Dynamic Host Configuration Protocol (DHCP) to assign IP addresses to devices connected to the network. Domain Name System (DNS) servers are responsible for managing default domain names, Network Time Protocol (NTP) servers, and IP routing using UDP ports 67 and 68.

The most important aspect of DHCP is the assignment of IP addresses to systems, referred to as a *DHCP lease*. Listed below are several of the characteristics of these servers and some areas of value they provide network forensic investigators.

1. Leases are not Permanent
2. Different IP Addresses are Issued Over Time
3. The Duration of the Lease is Configurable
4. **TIP**: Examine **all** DHCP Logs
5. Map all IP Addresses to the System
6. Search by Date for IP Addresses
7. Search all Dates for MAC Addresses

Microsoft DHCP: Server 2003

Logging is enabled by default on Microsoft servers, and a number of fields have been added to log files over time (2003, 2008, 2012). Microsoft Server 2003 logs seven primary data logs that are of interest to investigators. It is important for network investigators to realize that older versions of severs such as this will still be encountered in the field. Listed below are the seven primary data logs captured by MS Server 2003.

1. Event ID
2. Date
3. Time
4. Description
5. Host Name
6. IP Address
7. MAC Address

Microsoft DHCP: Server 2008

Windows Server 2008 added an additional six fields to its log files, for a total of 13 fields. Once again, it is important for network investigators to realize that older versions of severs such as this will still be encountered in the field. Listed below are the six additional data logs added by MS Server 2008.

1. User Name
2. Transaction ID
3. Q Result
4. Probation Time
5. Correlation ID
6. DHCID

Microsoft DHCP: Server 2012

Windows Server 2012 added an additional five fields to its log files, bringing the total number of log fields to 18. These additional log fields provide useful information for network forensic investigators.

1. Vendor Class (HEX)
2. Vendor Class (ASCII)
3. User Class (HEX)
4. User Class (ASCII)
5. Relay Agent Information

Microsoft DHCP: Server 2016

Windows Server 2016 is the seventh release of the Windows operating system developed as part of the Windows NT family of operating systems concurrently with Windows 10. In addition to providing new layers of security the release also included a number of new and updated features.

1. Active Directory Federation Services
2. A Cloud-Ready Application Platform
3. Docker Integration and Server Containers
4. Nested Virtualization (VM's within VM's)

Microsoft DHCP: Server 2019

Windows Server 2019 is the latest version of the Windows Server operating system by Microsoft as part of the Windows NT family of operating systems. In an effort to provide users with enhanced levels of security – and system administrators with a more "user-friendly" interface – a wide variety of upgraded features were included in the release. A few of the significant features are listed below.

1. Windows Admin Center (Based on *Project Honolulu*)
2. Windows Defender Advanced Threat Protection
3. A Desktop GUI (Graphical User Interface)
4. A Windows Subsystem on Linux
5. Automated Client Connectivity
    a. *DirectAccess*
    b. *Always On VPN*

Microsoft DHCP Considerations

Investigators should be aware of several considerations and restrictions specific to Microsoft DHCP servers. The first issue to be aware of is that the "date" and "time" fields in Microsoft DHCP logs are generated in local time, a challenge when correlating a series of geographical dispersed log files.

The second issue to be aware of is that DHCP logs overwrite themselves every week by design. Because most incidents go undetected for longer than a week, try to coordinate with IT staff to ensure logs are recorded and preserved.

Domain Name System (DNS) Servers

The Domain Name System (DNS) is a system that stores information primarily about host names and contains a wide variety of information useful to network investigators. In addition to looking up (resolving) host names to determine IP addresses – client resolution uses UDP port 53, zone transfer uses TCP port 53 – DNS servers can also initiate TCP / IP sessions.

The DNS resolution process, and the logs it generates, is an important source of evidence in a forensic investigation. Listed below are a number of useful leads that can be gathered using DNS servers.

1. The Host Name Requesting the Resolution
2. The IP Address of the Host Making the Request
3. The Result of the Resolution (Answering IP)
4. Determining Victimized Hosts
5. Finding Hosts with Active Malware
6. Answering Questions about Timelines

Network-Level DNS Logging

Local DNS logging cannot log both queries and responses, making application-level logging infeasible and impractical. Network-based solutions (such as *DNSCAP*) are much more practical for enterprise logging, as they can log both queries and responses, as well as monitor specific DNS traffic. Network-level logging is also a good solution for monitoring limited numbers of network traffic egress points.

The log files are outputted as PCAP or DIG-style messages, making them very user-friendly to access and analyze. As a word of caution, in Bind 9 and Microsoft DNS, the DNS answer generates log records spanning dozens of lines, generating huge log files. In these cases, applying filters properly will save investigators much valuable time and effort.

Enterprise Management Applications

Enterprise management applications are third-party software management and/or inventory tools Created to control and/or audit applications installed on a network. While not specifically designed for security purpose, these tools possess functionality that may prove to be exceptionally beneficial to network investigators.

Additionally, because attackers will likely run tools and malware on a compromised system, these applications (such as LANDesk's *Software Management Suite* and Symantec's *Altiris Client Management*) can provide insight into attacker activities.

LANDesk Software Management Suite

This tool is a popular third-party application for managing and controlling software inventory on a network. Its primary use is Software License Monitoring (SLM), but it has several capabilities that make it a valuable tool for network investigators. Listed below are five higher-level functions performed by LANDesk which make it useful in forensic investigations at the network-level.

1. Tracks the Application Execution History
2. Logs the Date and Time the Application Executed
3. Logs the File Attributes of the Executables
4. Logs the User Account that Ran the Executable
5. Retains Records if an Application is Deleted

LANDesk Registry Keys

The LANDesk Management Suite stores information about software execution in the Windows SOFTWARE registry hive. Listed below are seven LANDesk registry keys that may prove to be of specific interest when conducting network forensic investigations.

1. Current Duration   (REG_BINARY)
2. Current User   (REG_SZ)
3. First Started   (REG_BINARY)
4. Last Duration   (REG_BINARY)
5. Last Started   (REG_BINARY)
6. Total Duration   (REG_BINARY)
7. Total Runs   (REG_DWORD)

LANDesk Target Information

Forensic Investigators can benefit knowing what applications are running (or have been run) on a network or system. This holds especially true when building attack timelines and scoping the incident itself. Listed below are seven capabilities and categories of data which may prove to be especially useful during the investigation.

1. Detect Evidence of Intrusion
2. Identify Known Names of Malware
3. Frequency Analysis on "Total Runs"
4. Identify Suspicious Paths of Execution
5. Timeline Analysis and Date of the Compromise
6. Identify Suspicious Usernames
7. Identify Executables Deleted from System

Symantec Altiris Client Management

This tool is an enterprise endpoint management solution used for performance monitoring (and optional application metering). The logs generated by this solution contain much more information about the executables run on a system than the LANDesk registry keys.

The functionality of this solution includes the logging of application execution history and identifying evidence of system compromise. Critical artifacts are stored in the *AeXAMInventory Log*.

Symantec Target Information

The techniques previously described for LANDesk Software Management Suite also apply to the Altiris application metering logs. Listed below are a number of capabilities available with this solution that may prove useful during network investigations.

1. **Executables with No Version Information**: There are a few instances in which application updates are released without version information. However, this is not the norm. Malicious actors will frequently strip version information from executables to defeat signature-based security devices.

2. **Records Version in PE Headers**: The headers of Portable Executable files typically contain version information that is recorded by this solution. The contact and recording of blank headers may signal an Indicator of Compromise (IOC).

3. **Identify Unknown Malware on System**: In addition to known signatures for malware, malicious files can at times be identified by their size (which is detected and logged). For example, malware "backdoors" are typically less than one megabyte in size.

Antivirus (AV) Software

Some form of antivirus software is ubiquitous in virtually every enterprise environment. Most antivirus solutions possess a verbose logging capability which may prove to be a vital source of evidence during network investigations. However, AV solutions do have a few significant limitations.

Antivirus software will rarely detect all malicious programs an attacker tries to use on a system. If no effective signature for malware exists, the executable will go undetected by the system. The value of AV is well-established but paints an incomplete picture at best for network investigators.

Antivirus (AV) Quarantine

The purpose of antivirus quarantine is threat removal; the AV program encodes the suspected malicious file and stores it so it cannot execute on the system. Each antivirus product has its own method for encoding the quarantine files, some of which are created using complicated proprietary formats.

It serves a useful purpose in that legitimate programs mistakenly identified as malicious are not inadvertently deleted from systems, and it can also serve as a valuable tool to preserve evidence. However, many AV solutions are set to delete detected files by default, potentially destroying valuable evidence.

Network investigators involved with ongoing incidents should work with AV administrators to create policies for quarantining suspected files prior to deletion. With proper understanding of how the antivirus engine quarantines files, malware can be recovered from a compromised system and be examined for additional Indicators of Compromise.

Symantec Log Files

Symantec Endpoint Protection (SEP) is one of the most common antivirus suites investigators will encounter. The logs can provide valuable information to investigators even when errors in scanning make them appear to be less than useful.

For example, the antivirus product will log an error (because it cannot read an encrypted file) that includes the file name and path; that encrypted file may be malware.

Unfortunately, an antivirus solution may see none, some, or all of the programs attackers attempt to execute. Listed below are several SEP log characteristics and the benefits associated with those logs.

1. Logs are Stored in Plain Text
2. Stored in Comma Delimited Format (Exportable)
3. Easy to Examine and Parse
4. Current Version: Over 60 Log Fields
5. Logs the File in the Logs Directory
6. Logs in the Windows Application Event Log
7. SEP Events: "Event ID 51"
8. Logs the Description of Detection Signature
9. Logs the Full Path of the Associated File
10. Quarantine File Extension: ".VBN"
11. Creates Two .VBN Files for Each Quarantine
12. VBN 01: File Metadata
13. VBN 02: Encoded Copy Original File

McAfee Log Files

McAfee VirusScan Enterprise is a popular antivirus suite that stores log files locally on client / host even when connected to a management server. McAfee also provides a threat intelligence portal where analysts can obtain more detailed information about threats detected by VirusScan. Listed below are six log files that are of interested to network investigators, and characteristics of those log files as well.

1. AccessProtectionLog.txt
2. BufferOverflowProtectionLog.txt
3. MirrorLog.txt
4. OnAccessScanLog.txt   (Primary Interest)
5. OnDemandScanLog.txt   (Primary Interest)
6. UpdateLog.txt

These six logs are stored in the Log Directory. Two of these logs – *OnAccessScanLog.txt* and *OnDemandScanLog.txt* – may prove to be especially useful as they can provide evidence of quarantined or deleted files. These logs are also simultaneously stored in the Windows Application Event Log as "McAfee Event: Event ID 258" originating from the McAfee source "McLogEvent."

Trend Micro Office Scan

Trend Micro Office Scan is an antivirus suite commonly encountered by investigators when responding to enterprise incidents. It can remotely managed, store evidence on the client / host, and store information regarding detected threats. Log files are generated in plain text, making the seven included log values easy to access and analyze.

Listed below are the seven log fields that provide the most benefit for investigators. The details of the log fields are described in the Trend Micro Office *Scan 10 Report Objects Reference Guide*.

1. Date   (YYYYMMDD)
2. Time: Client Local Time   (HHMM)
3. Infection Name   (Name of Signature)
4. Scan Results   (Presented as Codes)
5. Scan Type   (Presented as Codes)
6. Not Used   (Unused Fields)
7. Path   (Path to Infected File)

Web Server Overview

Web servers are used to deliver most of the Internet's contact; forensic investigators will often encounter these servers during investigations. Investigators must understand web protocols in order to identify relevant configuration and log files. Web servers receive and respond to requests from clients, such as web browsers, using the Hypertext Transfer Protocol (HTTP).

The two versions of web servers most commonly encountered are the Apache HTTP Server and the Microsoft Internet Information

Services (IIS) Server. Listed below are several useful facts for this web server overview.

1. "GET" Requests Retrieve Data
2. "POST" Requests Upload Data
3. HTTP: TCP Port 80
4. HTTPS: TCP Port 443 (SSL)
5. Can be Configured for Virtual Host Capability
6. Can Host Potentially Thousands of Websites
7. RISK: Potential Impact on Unrelated Websites

Web Server Evidence

There are two primary sources of evidence derived from web servers: log files and the web server content. It should be a relief to network forensic investigators to find out that both the Apache HTTP Server and the Microsoft Internet Information Services (IIS) Server generate logs in plain text.

Listed below are six categories of information that may prove useful to investigators when reviewing web server logs.

1. Requests During a Specified Time
2. Requests to and from IP Addresses
3. Requests for Specific URL's
4. Requests Containing User and/or Agent Strings
5. Statistical Analysis and Information Flow
6. Identification of Anomalous Activity

Database Servers

Databases are a critical part of most modern enterprises, and at times not obvious due to their integration with other products. It is important for network forensic investigators to develop a good working relationship with the enterprise database administrator who will be assisting the Incident Response Team.

Data and log analysis should be avoided on production servers at all times – one small mistake can crash a server – and working in a live response environment is risky enough. It is a standard (and better) practice to image the database server and conduct all analysis of the image on a separate system. Listed below are four logs that may prove to be of unique interest to investigators when analyzing database servers.

1. Client Connection Logs
2. System Error Logs
3. User Query Logs
4. Database Storage Logs

DOMAIN 03

Overview of Common Network Services

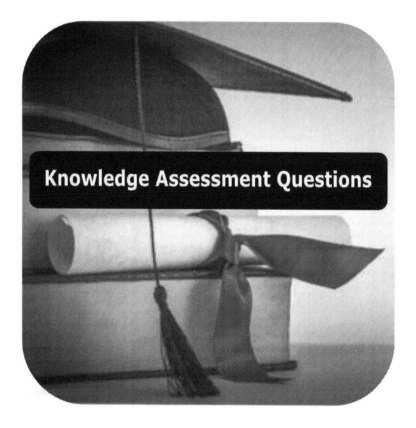

Knowledge Assessment Questions

The following knowledge assessment questions are presented in true / false, multiple choice, and fill-in-the-blank formats. The correct answers are provided in an Answer Key at the end of this text. These questions may or may not be presented on the actual certification exam.

Domain 03: Knowledge Assessment Questions

Most enterprises utilize _____ to assign IP addresses to devices connected to the network.

A. Internet Service Providers

B. Dynamic Host Configuration Protocol

C. Network Switches

D. Domain Name System

E. All of the Above

Which of the statements listed below is **not** a functionality of the LANDesk Software Management Suite?

A. Logs Date and Time the Application Executed

B. Tracks the Application Execution History

C. Records are Purged when the Application is Deleted

D. Documents the File Attributes of Executables

E. All of the Above

Logging is enabled by default on _____, and a number of fields have been added to log files over time.

A. Linux Servers

B. MAC OS X Servers

C. Microsoft Servers

D. Bind 9 Servers

E. All of the Above

Which McAfee log file in the list provided below provides the forensic investigator with the most useful and relevant information during Incident Response actions?

A. AccessProtectionLog.txt

B. MirrorLog.txt

C. OnAccessScanLog.txt

D. UpdateLog.txt

E. All of the Above

An issue for forensic investigators to be aware of is that the "date" and "time" fields in Microsoft Dynamic Host Configuration Protocol logs are generated in _____ time.

A. Eastern Standard Time

B. Greenwich Mean Time

C. Coordinated Universal Time

D. Local Time

E. None of the Above

Which of the statements listed below is a functionality and/or characteristic of standard Web Servers?

A. Uses POST Requests to Retrieve Data

B. Provides HTTP: UDP Port 80

C. Provides HTTPS: TCP Port 433 (SSL)

D. Configurable for Virtual Host Capability

E. All of the Above

There are three primary sources of evidence derived from database server log files available to forensic investigators: Client Connection Logs, User Query Logs, and _____.

A. System Error Logs

B. ARP Table Logs

C. Network Address Translation Log

D. Message Relay Log

E. All of the Above

Which of the statements listed below is **not** a functionality of Trend Micro Office Scan Antivirus Suite?

A. Stores Evidence Centrally on Domain Controllers

B. Can be Remotely Managed

C. Stores Information about Detected Threats

D. Log Files are Generated in Plain Text

E. All of the Above

Domain 03: *Overview of Common Network Services*

Symantec quarantine files are stored in a proprietary format with a .VBN extension and includes the file metadata and _____.
A. Encoded Original
B. UTC Time Stamp
C. Malware Version
D. Malware Creation Date
E. All of the Above

Which of the statements listed below is **not** a functionality of a Domain Name System (DNS) server?
A. Look Up (Resolve) Host Names
B. Assign Device MAC Addresses
C. Determine IP Addresses
D. Initiate TCP / IP Sessions
E. All of the Above

Web servers are typically configured to utilize Port 80 for HTTP traffic and Port _____ for HTTPS traffic (Secure Socket Layer).
A. 25
B. 23
C. 443
D. 143
E. None of the Above

Which Database Server log file in the list provided below provides the forensic investigator with the most useful and relevant information during Incident Response actions?
A. Client Connection Logs
B. System Error Logs
C. User Query Logs
D. Database Storage Logs
E. All of the Above

Domain 03: *Overview of Common Network Services*

The most important aspect of DHCP is the assignment of IP addresses to systems, called a DHCP lease.
1. True
2. False

An issue to be aware of is that the "date" and "time" fields in Microsoft DHCP logs are generated in the Coordinated Universal Time (UTC) format that is difficult to understand.
1. True
2. False

The Domain Name System (DNS) is a system that stores information primarily about host names.
1. True
2. False

In many instances, the antivirus product will log an error (because it cannot read an encrypted file) that includes the file size and type of malware family from which it is derived.
1. True
2. False

McAfee provides a threat intelligence portal where analysts can obtain more detailed information about threats detected by VirusScan.
1. True
2. False

Web servers receive and respond to requests from clients, such as web browsers, using the File Transfer Protocol (FTP).
1. True
2. False

DOMAIN 04

Fundamentals of
Secure Network Architecture

Introduction to Secure Architecture

In order to understand what secure architecture is, it is important to understand its origin and subsequent evolution. In the early days, the focus was on network security; protecting the perimeter from external threats. As networks became more secure attacks on infrastructure became more prevalent and the focus shifted to infrastructure security.

As infrastructure has become more secure attack methodologies changed again which shifted the focus to application security. Listed below are several frameworks that have contributed to the evolution of network security.

1. Zachman Framework (1987)
2. NIST Framework (1989)
3. TOGAF Framework (1995)
4. SABSA Framework (2007)

Zachman Framework

The *Zachman Framework* is an enterprise ontology that provides a fundamental and formalized structure for enterprise architecture. It presents a two-dimensional classification system that organizes and analyzes data based on two schemata. The first schema addresses general interrogatives: who, what, when, where, and why.

The second schema addresses the concepts of *reification* (the process of treating an immaterial idea as a material thing) and *instantiation* (providing an instance or material evidence in support of a concept). The framework considers users of data and issues with data but does not imply a specific technical methodology.

TOGAF Framework

The *Open Group Architecture Framework* (TOGAF) is a framework that provides an approach for developing an enterprise architecture. It is intended to serve as a high-level approach to design. The framework defines system components, provides recommended standards, and establishes a common vocabulary. It addresses four architectural domains (business, information, application, and technology) referred to as *TOGAF Pillars*. Its high-level approach can make it difficult to implement.

SABSA Framework

The *Sherwood Applied Business Security Architecture* (SABSA) is a framework for security architecture and service management. It is both a model and methodology for developing risk-driven architectures and infrastructure security solutions. It was founded on business analysis principles to support critical business functions. It is not widely accepted and has little relevance outside of network security.

Reference Security Architecture

A *reference security architecture* is a document which provides recommended integrations of products and services to form a solution. The reference architecture embodies industry best practices, typically suggesting the optimal delivery method for specific technologies. Listed below are several focus areas addressed in the document.

1. Border Protection
2. Detection Services
3. Content Control Services
4. Configuration Management
5. Identity and Access Management
6. Application Security
7. Software Development Life Cycle
8. Physical Security Technology
9. Cryptographic Security
10. Auditing Processes

Border Protection

Border protection is typically thought of as the component technological devices that provide security at the network layer. Listed below are several focus areas that should be considered when addressing network border protection.

1. Network Zoning
2. The Testing and Development Environment
3. The Quality Assurance (QA) and Mirror Environment
4. The Production Environment
5. The Desktop Environment
6. Internal and External Demilitarized Zones (DMZ's)
7. Bring Your Own Device (BYOD) Integration

Detection Services

Detection services are those capabilities put in place with the specific focus of attempting to detect incidents in the process of occurring. Listed below are several focus areas that should be considered when addressing network detection services.

1. IDS and NIDS (Intrusion Detection Systems)
2. IPS and NIPS (Intrusion Protection Systems)
3. Firewalls and Routers
4. Network Access Controls (NAC's)
5. Event Monitoring
6. Dashboards and GRC Platforms (Governance, Risk, and Compliance)

Content Control Services

Content control services are those capabilities put in place to monitor and control the internal and external data flow within a network. Listed below are several focus areas that should be considered when addressing content control services.

1. Data Loss Prevention (DLP)
2. Whitelisting and Blacklisting
3. Content Filtering
4. Web Activity Monitoring
5. Anti-Virus Services
6. Anti-Spam Services
7. File Transfers (FTP and SFTP)

Configuration Management

Configuration management is implemented to ensure that a solution remains in the configuration for which is was originally intended. Listed below are several focus areas that should be considered when addressing network configuration management.

1. Hardening
2. Golden Images
3. Virtualization
4. Patch Management
5. Vulnerability Assessment
6. Group Policy Objects (GPO's)

Identity and Access Management

Identity and access management (IAM) consists of policies and technologies to ensure the proper people have the appropriate access to resources. Listed below are several focus areas that should be considered when addressing identity and access management.

1. Provisioning
2. Credentials
3. Access Management
4. Data Repositories
5. Federation

Software Development Life Cycle (SDLC)

The *application layer* is where most vulnerabilities are presented and the greatest effort in reducing vulnerabilities is expended. The *Software Development Life Cycle* (SDLC) is a process used by the software industry to design, develop and test applications. Listed below are the six phases of the SDLC.

1. Planning and Analysis
2. Design and Development
3. Testing and Evaluation
4. Deployment
5. Monitoring and Maintenance
6. Decommission and Disposal

Physical Security Technology

Physical security has become increasingly reliant on technology to function and plays an important role in security architecture. Listed below are several focus areas that should be considered when addressing physical security technology.

1. Physical Access Control
2. Video Surveillance
3. Physical Intrusion Detection
4. Visitor Management
5. Communication Systems
6. Central Management Systems
7. Environmental Controls

Cryptographic Services

Cryptographic services are complex technological components of security architecture that are crucial for the protection of information assets. Listed below are several focus areas that should be considered when addressing cryptographic services.

Domain 04: *Fundamentals of Secure Network Architecture*

1. Data at Rest
2. Data in Motion
3. Certificate Authority
4. Certificate Validation
5. Certificate Revocation and Lists (CRL's)
6. High Security Models
7. Tokenization

Auditing Services

Although *auditing* is not technical by nature it must take into consideration technology standards an organization is required to meet. Listed below are several focus areas that should be considered when addressing auditing services.

1. Risk Registers (Security)
2. Risk Registers (Architectural)
3. Compliance Scanning
4. Industry Standards
5. Security Certifications

Architecture Design Document (ADD)

The *architecture design document* (ADD) details the projects' end state and the steps required for the solution to be implemented successfully. It is typically segmented into four categories based on the *TOGAF Pillars* listed below.

1. Business Architecture
2. Information Architecture
3. Application Architecture
4. Technology Architecture

Business Architecture

The *business architecture* identifies and defines the organizations' strategy, governance, structure, goals, and key business processes. The objective is to create a governance model that is in alignment with the organization. Regardless of the aspects of the business included in this document, the four areas of focus listed below should be included.

1. Entire Cost and Impact
2. Process Flows
3. RACI Chart Components
4. Change Management and Updates

Information Architecture

Information architecture describes the structure of an organizations' logical and physical data assets and data management resources. This document generally addresses the focus areas listed below.

1. Solution Information
2. Structure of the Data
3. Structure of the Database
4. System Information
5. Criticality of the Data
6. Classification of the Data
7. CRUD Matrix of Permissions (Create, Read, Update, and Delete)

Application Architecture

Application architecture documents solution deployments, system interactions, and their relationships to core business processes. This document generally addresses the focus areas listed below.

1. COTS Applications (Commercial Off-the-Shelf)

2. Custom Applications
3. Hybrid Applications
4. Web Application Firewalls
5. Input Validation
6. Session Considerations
7. Exception Handling

Technology Architecture

Technology architecture describes the hardware, software, and network infrastructure needed to support the deployment of a solution. Several common components of this document are listed below.

1. Network Components
2. Server Components
3. Database Components
4. Application Server Components
5. System Management Tools
6. Back-Up Components
7. Endpoint Components

Zero Trust Networks: Assertions

Modern networks and usage patterns no longer resemble those that made traditional perimeter defense a practical solution years ago. The *Zero Trust Model* rejects the concept of perimeter defense and instead embraces the idea that no perimeter exists and all components of the network must be equally defended. It always assumes the network is hostile, threats are both internal and external, and threats are always active.

Due to these assertions locality cannot decide the level of trust for actors in the network. Every person and device must be authenticated and authorized at all times. The model uses multisource and dynamic policies to accomplish these objectives.

Zero Trust Network Flows

The perimeter model attempts to build a wall between trusted and untrusted sources; the zero trust model assumes all actors are threats. Given that assumption, network flows are scrutinized at all times. The following is a general overview of the network flow process.

The user and the device are authenticated based on temporal, geographical, and behavioral attributes. A *trust score* is computed and the results are bonded to form an *agent*. The *control plane* (security policy) signals the *data plane* (network resources) that the network flow will be allowed to take place.

The control plane verifies the device and application are using proper encryption protocols and the network flow is authorized and logged.

If at any time during this process the trust score fails to meet a predefined threshold, the control plane will prevent the network flow from occurring and the failed attempt will be logged.

Zero Trust Network Agents

It is insufficient to treat the user and device separately because policy often needs to consider the two together to enforce behavior. A network agent is the term given to known data regarding network actors such as users, devices, and applications.

While information regarding network actors is maintained in persistent storage, the agent is formed "on demand." When a request is made it evaluates the known data, variable attributes, and trust score against the security policy to make an authorization decision.

Unlike a typical perimeter-based system in which trust is granted users and devices based on roles and rules, trust scores in a zero trust network are dynamic and volatile. The flexibility of a variable trust system allows enforcement policies to be implemented when encountering unique and unknown threats.

Zero Trust Privilege Considerations

By considering all details of an access attempt, the determination of authorization is more granular than a simple binary response. The level of privilege granted on a zero trust network is highly dynamic, changing in direct proportion to trust scores and circumstances.

The static privilege of a traditional network can be risky. It can be too rigid and defined to adequately address network threats. It can be too loosely defined for security policies to be adequately asserted. Finally, it can become accumulated without proper controls and management.

In addition to considering the assigned privilege of users and devices on the network, this model also evaluates the attributes listed in the examples below.

1. **Temporal Attributes**: The time of day a user or device is attempting to access the network.

2. **Geographical Attributes**: The location from which the user or device is attempting to access the network.

3. **Behavioral Attributes**: The assets and resources the user or device is attempting to access on the network.

Trust Agent Data Fields (Part I)

The granularity of data stored within a trust agent can vary based on the needs of the organization and maturity of the system. Listed below are a number of data fields that may be used to evaluate users of a network.

1. Agent Trust Score
2. User Trust Score
3. User Role and Group Role
4. User Place of Residence
5. User Authentication Method

Trust Agent Data Fields (Part II)

Device data populated during the procurement process is more trusted than device data reported back from an agent running on it. As a result, trust scores for devices vary as well. Listed below are a number of data fields that may be used to evaluate devices on a network.

1. Device Trust Score
2. Device Manufacturer
3. TPM Manufacturer and Version
4. Current Device Location
5. IP Address

Zero Trust Networks: Disadvantages

There are several potential shortcomings, risks, and attack vectors associated with a zero trust network that can undermine its utility. The examples listed below can potentially compromise zero trust networks due to their lack of focus on perimeter security.

1. Identity Theft
2. Endpoint Enumeration
3. Untrusted Computing Platform
4. Social Engineering
5. Physical Coercion
6. Invalidation (No Longer Authorized)
7. Control Plane Security

[This page intentionally left blank]

DOMAIN 04

Fundamentals of Secure Network Architecture

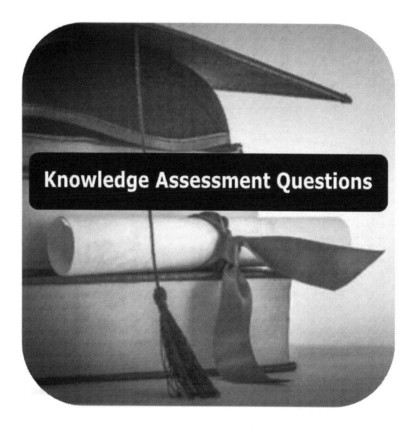

The following knowledge assessment questions are presented in true / false, multiple choice, and fill-in-the-blank formats. The correct answers are provided in an Answer Key at the end of this text. These questions may or may not be presented on the actual certification exam.

Domain 04: Knowledge Assessment Questions

Which choice below is a characteristic of *The Open Group Architecture Framework* that provides an approach for developing enterprise architecture?

A. Mid-Level Design Approach

B. Provides a Unique Vocabulary

C. Created by John Zachman

D. Defines System Components

E. None of the Above

Modern networks and usage patterns no longer resemble those that made traditional _____ a practical solution years ago.

A. Perimeter Defense

B. Compensating Controls

C. Logging Reports

D. Alerting Systems

E. None of the Above

Select the best choice below for the following definition: "*An enterprise ontology that provides a fundamental and formalized structure for enterprise architecture.*"

A. COBIT Framework

B. TOGAF Framework

C. Zachman Framework

D. ITIL Framework

E. None of the Above

The _____ identifies and defines the organizations' strategy, governance, structure, goals, and key business processes.

A. Data Architecture

B. Business Architecture

C. Technology Architecture

D. Application Architecture

E. None of the Above

Domain 04: *Fundamentals of Secure Network Architecture*

Which choice below is a potential risk and/or attack vector associated with Zero Trust Networks that can undermine its utility?

A. Data Plane Security
B. Control Plane Security
C. Server Enumeration
D. Trusted Computing Platform
E. None of the Above

_____ is/are complex technological components of security architecture that are crucial for the protection of information assets.

A. Physical Security
B. Content Control Services
C. Cryptographic Services
D. Detection Services
E. None of the Above

Select the best choice below for the following definition: "*Describes the hardware, software, and network infrastructure needed to support the deployment of a solution.*"

A. Technology Architecture
B. Business Architecture
C. Data Architecture
D. Application Architecture
E. None of the Above

The _____ is where most vulnerabilities are presented and the greatest effort in reducing vulnerabilities is expended.

A. Network Layer
B. Session Layer
C. Data Link Layer
D. Application Layer
E. None of the Above

Domain 04: *Fundamentals of Secure Network Architecture*

Which choice below is one of the six phases comprising the Software Development Life Cycle (SDLC)?

A. Purchasing

B. Operating

C. Securing

D. Planning

E. None of the Above

A(n) _____ is a document which provides recommended integrations of products and services to form a solution.

A. Reference Security Architecture

B. Software Architecture Document

C. Enterprise Architecture Document

D. Architecture Design Document

E. None of the Above

Select the best choice below for the following definition: "*Complex technological components of security architecture that are crucial for the protection of information assets.*"

A. Identity and Access Management

B. Content Control Services

C. Cryptographic Services

D. Configuration Management

E. None of the Above

The _____ documents solution deployments, system interactions, and their relationships to core business processes.

A. Data Architecture

B. Business Architecture

C. Technology Architecture

D. Application Architecture

E. None of the Above

Domain 04: *Fundamentals of Secure Network Architecture*

The TOGAF Framework is an enterprise ontology that provides a fundamental and formalized structure for enterprise architecture.
1. True
2. False

The granularity of data stored within a trust agent can vary based on the needs of the organization and maturity of the system.
1. True
2. False

Border protection is typically thought of as the component technological devices that provide security at the transport layer.
1. True
2. False

Technology architecture describes the hardware, software, and network infrastructure needed to support the deployment of a solution.
1. True
2. False

Identity management is implemented to ensure that a solution remains in the configuration for which is was originally intended.
1. True
2. False

The perimeter model attempts to build a wall between trusted and untrusted sources; zero trust assumes all actors are malicious.
1. True
2. False

DOMAIN 05

Incident Response Management

Incident Response Management

Prior to studying and engaging in the concept of Incident Response management, the network investigator would benefit from understanding the following truths:

FACT:

Most of the challenges to Incident Response are non-technical.

FACT:

The core principles of investigating a computer security incident does not differ from a non-technical investigation.

Common Computer Security Incidents

All suspicious events occurring on a computer system or network should be viewed as potential incidents until proven otherwise by the Incident Response Team. A few incidents likely to be encountered which qualify as potential incidents are listed below.

1. **Data Theft**: Personally Identifiable Information (PII), Protected Health Information (PHI), legitimate email accounts, and sensitive documents.

2. **Financial Theft**: Fraud, embezzlement, credit cards, card verification values (CVV's), bank account numbers, and any sensitive data relating to organizational finances.

3. **Non-Technical Criminal Acts**: Criminal activities that have now been made easier to execute because of the anonymity of the Internet include blackmail, extortion, stalking, and cyber bullying.

4. **Unauthorized Access**: This type of activity includes users with legitimate permission to access resources of a system

or network but exceed their assigned access levels without express authorization.

5. **Malicious Code**: Malicious code introduced into a system or network, intentionally or accidently, includes examples such as malware, spyware, and ransomware.

6. **Unauthorized Materials**: Any materials users of a system or network download, upload, or transfer that are illegal (by law) or unauthorized (by policy) may include pirated files protected by copyright or pornographic images.

Initial Goals of Incident Response

Using both technical and non-technical information obtained during the Incident Response investigation, network forensic investigators will have the ability to develop and implement an effective remediation strategy. There are six initial goals which are especially critical to the initial phase of the investigation.

1. **Determine the Initial Attack Vector**: By establishing the initial attack vector, investigators can identity exploitable vulnerabilities in the network and/or personnel within the organization subjected to social engineering actions.

2. **Determine the Tools and Methods Used**: In many cases, the ability to identify the tools and methods of the attackers will help determine their operational capabilities and their possible motivation for compromising the network.

3. **Identify the Affected Systems**: Identifying the affected systems will allow investigators to thoroughly scope the severity of the incident, determine possible goals of the attackers, and prepare for an effective remediation once the incident has been resolved.

4. **Conduct a Damage Assessment**: Once affected systems have been identified, a damage assessment will reveal any

stolen data or funds, modified data or systems, and even serve to gauge potential reputational damage.

5. **Determine if the Incident is Ongoing**: If an incident is determined to be ongoing – contingent upon the severity and damage of the incident – an investigation prior to the implementation of remediation actions may provide valuable intelligence to the Incident Response Team.

6. **Establish a Timeline for the Incident**: In addition to properly scoping the severity of the incident and potential damage inflicted by the attacker, an incident timeline will assist in developing remediation strategies and possible legal actions against those malicious actors involved.

Incident Response Team Composition

The composition of the Incident Response Team will be highly diverse and represent specialized capabilities in both technical and non-technical disciplines. Representatives from cross-functional Incident Response Teams may include, but are not limited to:

1. Legal Counsel   (External and Internal)
2. Compliance Officers (All Relevant Industries)
3. IT Support Staff   (Help Desk and Call Center)
4. Infrastructure Staff (System and Network)
5. Management Staff   (All Organizational Units)
6. Human Resources   (External and Internal)
7. Public Relations   (External and Internal)

Incident Response Team Considerations

The ability to create and maintain an Incident Response Team will vary from organization to organization based on numerous factors such as available budget, personnel and experience. In the event external resources must be secured, consider contracting those resources through legal counsel to ensure all communications and negotiations are reasonably protected from disclosure. A few of the issues to be considered when creating an Incident Response Team include:

1. **Cost of Maintaining the Team**: Is it cost effective based on the size of the organization?

2. **Culture of Outsourcing**: Does the organization tend to outsource specialized capabilities instead of investing time, money, and resources to creating the capability internally?

3. **Mandated by Regulation**: Is the organization subjected to regulations and compliance dictating the existence of an Incident Response Team?

4. **Level of Experience**: Does the organization possess the adequate staff and training budget to ensure investigations can be handled by experienced personnel?

5. **Limited In-House Specialization**: Is the organizations' mission such that no need exists for expertise in Incident Response initiatives?

Vetting Team Members for Experience

Whether an organization possesses the personnel and budget to create an internal Incident Response Team, or determines that outsourcing is a more viable option, vetting the team candidates for requisite experience is critical. This experience includes, but is not limited to:

1. **Technological Investigations**: The candidate must have experience with investigations involving technology, not just investigations in separate disciplines. While candidates may possess superior investigative skills, lacking expertise in technology places them at a significant disadvantage.

2. **Computer Forensics**: The ability to examine and analyze forensic images secured from networks (live acquisition) or independent devices ("dead box") is critical to developing actionable leads and answering investigative questions.

3. **Network Traffic Analysis**: A knowledge of information flows with a network is vital when distinguishing normal behaviors from potential anomalies. Additionally, a working knowledge of traffic analysis software will enhance the process by facilitating efficient and effective automation.

4. **Relevant Industry Applications**: Every industry uses certain related software to manage every aspect of its operation. While vendors may change from organization to organization, the applications share commonality that will allow experienced investigators to quickly understand the functionality if they are familiar with industry applications.

5. **Enterprise IT Architecture**: Understanding enterprise architecture and general network topology provides a level of insight that allows investigators to identify many behavioral anomalies of standard network devices. If an investigator can identify anomalies against known and acceptable device behaviors, the remediation process can be greatly enhanced.

6. **Malicious Code Analysis**: Understanding functionality of a malicious code can very often reveal its purpose – as well as the motivation and intent of the attacker. Possessing this capability also removes the need to outsource this function to third-parties, which in many cases is neither desired nor feasible.

Vetting Team Members for Soft Skills

There is no such thing as a "perfect" Incident Response Team member. However, there are individuals who should never be considered for Incident Response because of a deficiency in their soft skills.

When considering candidates for an Incident Response Team – whether they are internal or external – a hiring manager should strive to recruit candidates demonstrating the following qualities:

Domain 05: *Incident Response Management*

1. **Highly Analytical**   (Critical Thinking Skills)
2. **Effective Communicator** (Technical and Non-Technical)
3. **Attention to Detail**   (Macro and Micro)
4. **Organized Approach**   (Structured and Systematic)
5. **Problem Solving**   (Demonstrable Successes)

Initial Response Interview Activities

When faced with the prospect of being victimized with a severe incident, the first emotional response is to act quickly. While that can be understandable, it is typically the least effective decision. Acting on incomplete and/or inaccurate information is far riskier than preparing a reasoned response based on factual data.

For this reason, conducting initial interviews with relevant parties prior to acting is critical. In all case, document all information gathered during these interviews. Listed below are a few likely candidates that may be considered for initial interviews.

1. **Person(s) Reporting Incident**: What role do they occupy within the organization, and what caused them to report this incident?

2. **IT / Technical Staff**: Have they validated the incident, source data for notification, and whether the source of the notification was human or automated?

3. **Organizational Personnel**: Although an action alerted an incident occurred, can unit personnel provide any context that identifies the alert as an anomaly as opposed to a "business as usual" event?

4. **Network Security Personnel**: Have logs associated with the potential incident been reviewed, from what source were the logs generated, and is there an established error rate documented for the reporting mechanisms?

Domain 05: *Incident Response Management*

Iterative Lead Gathering Process

The process followed by network investigators for gathering leads is not linear; it is cyclical and repetitive. Time and resources are typically in short supply, making the gathering of relevant facts and leads critical components of incident remediation.

It is important to avoid a fixation on malware; it is rarely an attacker's only goal to install malware, and once credentials are compromised malware becomes secondary to the process. Listed below are the high-level steps of the iterative lead gathering process.

1. Gather Initial Leads
2. Begin the Indicator of Compromise Creation Process
3. Deploy and Refine the Indicators of Compromise
4. Identify Systems of Interest
5. Collect all Relevant Evidence
6. Analyze the Collected Data for New Leads

Indicators of Compromise (IOC) Creation

Indicator of compromise creation is the process of documenting the characteristics and artifacts of an incident in a structured manner. The IOC documentation is then used as a foundation to create automated filters to generate additional relevant leads, discount potential false positive "hits," and relay alerts to security personnel based on established IOC parameters.

A few items to consider when creating Indicators of Compromise are listed below:

1. Working Directory Names
2. Output File Names
3. Login Attempts (Failed and Successful)
4. Persistence Mechanisms
5. IP Addresses
6. Domain Names

7. Malware Protocol Signatures

Indicators of Compromise (IOC) Deployment

One of the functional benefits of IOC deployment is the ability to employ automation to expedite the network scanning process. The majority of larger organizations license enterprise-level Incident Response platforms utilizing Visual Basic (VB) scripting or Windows Management Instrumentation. Whether working with commercial or non-commercial tools, the majority of solutions support Snort rules making the user interface much less complex.

While there are a number of network-level IOC solutions, the number of host-based solutions is restricted and limited. Two limitations to be aware of when considering host-based IOC's includes a lack of both accepted industry standards and free enterprise-level solutions.

Snort and Snort Rules

Snort rules help network forensic investigators in differentiating between normal internet activities and malicious activities in real time. Initially developed by Cisco, listed below are a few facts about Snort rules, capabilities, and characteristics with which a network investigator should be familiar.

1. Free Open Source IDS / IPS
2. Flexible Rule-Based Language
3. Keys on Signatures, Protocols, and Anomalies
4. Detects Malicious Network Activity
5. Uses Libpcap and Winpcap Libraries
6. Packet Logging and Inspection Capabilities

IOC: Identifying Systems of Interest

Prioritization of systems of interest during IOC investigations is based on numerous factors, not just the criticality of data and/or the business processes affected by the incident. Listed below are the six high-level steps network investigators will experience when conducting IOC investigations.

1. The IOC Generates Initial "Hits" (Alerts)
2. Perform an Initial Triage on the New Hits
3. Validate the Hit
4. Categorize the Hit for Reliability and Relevance
5. Categorize the Hit Based on Activity
6. Prioritize the Hit Based on Relevance

IOC: Process to Preserve Evidence

Limited time and resources result in limited evidence collection. Network investigators must use a system of prioritization to manage collection decisions, while at the same time ensuring that all evidence (live response, memory, and disk imaging) collected is preserved properly.

1. Minimize Changes to the System
2. Minimize Interaction Time with the System
3. Generate Appropriate Documentation

Live Response

Live response is the most common collection process utilized during network Incident Response when incursions are suspected and involves collecting data on live systems using automated tools. Both volatile and non-volatile evidence can be collected from any system of interest.

Typical information of value to network investigators includes process listings, network connections, list of file system objects, event logs, and registry contents. The three primary benefits of conducting a live response are listed below.

1. Confirmation of the System and/or Network Compromise
2. Determining the Compromise Methodology Details
3. Revealing Additional Leads and Evidence

Domain 05: *Incident Response Management*

Memory Collection

Memory collection is the least utilized method in incident response due to its limited ability to provide significant answers to high-level questions and root causes to problems. However, it does provide value to network investigators for the identification of active malware, and when faced with challenges such as those listed below.

1. Identify the Mechanisms Hiding Attack Activities
2. If the Investigator Cannot Obtain a Disk Image
3. Few Evidentiary Artifacts Remain on the Disk
4. Attacker Activity is Memory-Resident

Disk Imaging

When network investigators are responding to incidents in which intrusion is not suspected, disk imaging is a standard operating procedure. Drives are typically imaged in live mode when imaging is the only option; captured images tend to large and require a significant amount of time to gather. There are usually two primary benefits when imaging a live system:

1. Identify Many Malicious Actions Over Time
2. Provides Solutions for Many Unanswered Questions

Analyzing Data Evidence

Analyzing data is simply the examination of preserved evidence gathered for the purpose of answering investigative questions. It typically commands the largest amount of an investigators' time and is always documented in formal reports. Network investigators will typically conduct analysis on three categories of collected data.

1. Malware Analysis
2. Live Response Analysis
3. Forensic Examination Analysis

Malware Analysis

Most network incidents include the use of malware at some stage of the attack life cycle. Unfortunately, most organizations do not possess the budget, staff, or capability to have a dedicated malware analysis staff. Most malware reports are based on IOC results, and may include information regarding the description and general functionality of the malicious code.

Network investigators considering an in-house malware analysis capability must possess three distinct capabilities.

1. Capability to Triage Malware
2. Capability to Perform a Static Malware Analysis
3. Capability to Perform a Dynamic Malware Analysis

Live Response Analysis

Every organization should have a live response analysis capability to some degree. It is the most critical stage of any network investigation when suspicious activity is suspected but details are limited. The benefits of conducting live response analysis are twofold: an investigator can ascertain a "big picture" view of the incident as a whole while generating new leads relevant to the investigation. However, three serious risks exist:

1. A Portion of Attacker Activity may Possibly be Overlooked
2. Investigators can Mistakenly Dismiss Entire Systems
3. Impacts of Unauthorized Access by the Investigator

Forensic Examination Analysis

During traditional network investigations not involving intrusion, this portion of the investigation consumes the most time for the forensic investigators. Digital forensic investigators who are accustomed to working in workstation labs and operating on internal timelines may also find this analysis the most frustrating. Network investigators should be aware of five realities associated with this type of analysis.

1. It is a Focused and Time-Sensitive Task
2. There is Not Enough Time for a Thorough Examination
3. Create a Short List of Realistic Questions
4. Decide on the Best and Most Simplistic Approach
5. Execute Specific Tasks to Answer Specific Questions

Incident Remediation

Incident remediation is the ultimate goal of any Incident Response. It is typically initiated when the incident is determined to be in a "steady state," the point of time when established Indicators of Compromise (IOC) have stopped alerting to new and previously unknown events.

The remediation plan should consider all Incident Response Team factors including legal, business, political, and technical components. It is also critical to establish a formal communication protocol to ensure proper timing of remediation plan initiation for the following two reasons:

1. Start Too Soon: Malicious Attacker Activity may be Missed
2. Start Too Late: Attacker may Change TTP's and Impacts

Tracking Investigative Information

Network investigations must have a mechanism in place to easily track information and share it with ancillary Incident Response Teams in a timely manner. This data will be the first thing investigators will reference when any queries come from management and/or senior leadership. There are ten general categories of information listed below that should be tracked by Incident Response Teams engaged in network investigations.

1. Critical Data to any Aspect of Investigation
2. List of Collected Evidence
3. List of Affected Systems
4. List of any Files of Interest
5. List of Accessed and/or Stolen Data

6. Significant Attacker Activity
7. List of Network-Based Indicators of Compromise
8. List of Host-Based Indicators of Compromise
9. List of Compromised System Accounts
10. Ongoing Tasks and Requests for Team Members

Incident Response Reporting

Reports are a primary deliverable for any Incident Response Team and the Network Forensic Investigators involved in that effort. Creating great reports – which accurately document the results of undertaken efforts – takes time, patience, and practice.

An additional and often overlooked benefit of this process is reporting forces investigators to slow down, document findings in a structured format, verify evidence, and think with a "big picture" mindset.

There are three basic guidelines listed below to assist investigators in their report writing process.

1. **Write Formal Periodic Reports**: Waiting until the end of an incident to begin writing a formal report can virtually guarantee facts will be forgotten and critical details will be missed. When writing reports that may be subject to revision be based on newly discovered facts and evidence, label the report as "DRAFT."

2. **Use a Standardized Template**: Standardized templates make reporting easier for the investigators involved, ensure specific categories of facts are not overlooked, and provide a level of consistency that makes the report easier to read and understand by third-parties.

3. **Use Standardized Language Guidelines**: People will typically use different words to describe the same object (computer, laptop, machine, system). Enforcing language guidelines will increase consistency and help to reduce confusion and discrepancies.

[This page intentionally left blank]

DOMAIN 05

Incident Response Management

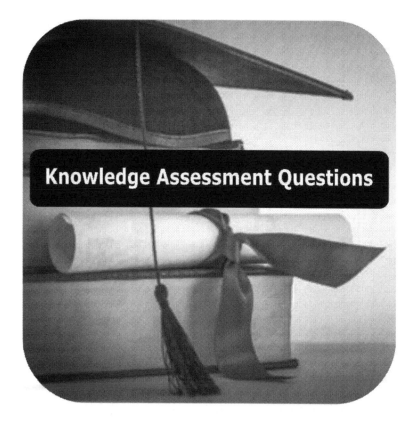

The following knowledge assessment questions are presented in true / false, multiple choice, and fill-in-the-blank formats. The correct answers are provided in an Answer Key at the end of this text. These questions may or may not be presented on the actual certification exam.

Domain 05: Knowledge Assessment Questions

The actions taken by a forensic network investigator when performing any kind of data analysis include _____.
A. Perform a Conversion and/or Naturalization
B. Obtain the Relevant Data
C. Select the Analysis Method
D. Define and Understand the Objectives
E. All of the Above

Which of the following options should forensic investigators not consider as a goal when responding to a network incident?
A. Identify the Affected Systems
B. Conduct a Damage Assessment
C. Determine the Initial Attack Vector
D. Identification of All Malware
E. All of the Above

Most of the challenges a forensic network investigator may face when responding to an Incident Response are _____.
A. Non-Technical
B. Unforeseeable
C. Financial and/or Budgetary
D. Disk Imaging
E. None of the Above

Which of the following representatives from the victim organization should be considered for participation on the Incident Response Team?
A. IT / IS Infrastructure
B. Business Management
C. Human Resources
D. Legal Counsel
E. All of the Above

The forensic investigator should view _____ as potential incidents until and investigation proves otherwise.

A. Data Theft

B. Financial Fraud

C. Suspicious Events

D. Malware and Ransomware

E. None of the Above

When developing an Incident Response Team capability within a victim organization, which of the following options should not be considered by a forensic investigator?

A. Cost of Team Maintenance

B. Scope of the Incident

C. Culture of Outsourcing

D. Investigative Capabilities

E. None of the Above

Forensic investigators should consider contracting external resources through _____ so that communications are reasonably protected from disclosure.

A. Established SLA's

B. Human Resources

C. Vendor Contracts

D. Legal Counsel

E. None of the Above

When vetting the soft skills of potential members of the Incident Response Team, which of the following should **not** be considered as a prerequisite for acceptance?

A. History of Promotion

B. Effective Communication

C. Highly Analytical

D. Success in Problem Solving

E. None of the Above

Domain 05: *Incident Response Management*

During traditional investigations not involving _____, the forensic examination analysis portion of the investigation consumes the most time.

A. Regulation and/or Compliance

B. Multiple Network Segments

C. Intrusion

D. Government Agencies

E. None of the Above

When planning the initial response interview activities, who should the forensic investigator include in the first round of interviews to be conducted?

A. Person(s) Reporting the Incident

B. IT and Technical Personnel

C. Business Unit Personnel

D. Network Security Log Personnel

E. All of the Above

Live response analysis is a critical part of the Incident Response process when network investigators observe suspicious activity but have limited _____.

A. Details

B. Time

C. Qualified Staff

D. Leadership Support

E. All of the Above

Which of the following is **not** a reason for a forensic investigator to pursue a memory collection strategy during live acquisition?

A. Identify Active Malware

B. Activity is Memory Resident

C. Answer High-Level Questions

D. Cannot Obtain a Disk Image

E. None of the Above

Domain 05: *Incident Response Management*

The core principles of investigating a computer security incident are inherently different from a non-technical investigation.

1. True
2. False

Indicators of Compromise (IOC) creation is the process of documenting the characteristics and the artifacts of an incident in a structured manner.

1. True
2. False

Acting on incomplete and/or inaccurate information is acceptable if a reasoned response based on factual data may take more time to investigate.

1. True
2. False

Snort rules help Incident Response investigators by differentiating between normal internet activities and malicious activities in real time.

1. True
2. False

Prioritization during an Indicator of Compromise investigation is based solely on the criticality of data and/or the critical business process affected by the compromise.

1. True
2. False

When responding to incidents in which intrusion is not suspected, disk imaging is a standard operating procedure.

1. True
2. False

DOMAIN 06

Investigative Principles and Lead Development

Understanding Elements of Proof

Every case type and investigation has its own considerations— whether the goal is litigation or developing a stronger security posture. Elements of proof serve to define the elements of a claim. Initially the driving claims a few and broad but develop in greater detail over time as the investigation evolves.

The focus of the investigation will be determined by the primary consumer of the report. The majority of investigations are led by legal teams with the responsibility to prove or disprove the driving claims. The Incident Response and Network Forensic Teams have the responsibility of pursuing investigative actions, collecting evidence, and acting in support of the legal mission.

Investigations of high importance will always generate a greater level of scrutiny for everyone on the team.

The Purpose of Investigations

An investigation is a systematic examination, typically with the purpose of identifying or verifying facts. It will attempt to answer one or all of the questions listed below.

1. WHO   (All Persons Involved)
2. WHERE   (All Relevant Locations Involved)
3. WHAT   (A Description of Factual Elements)
4. WHEN   (The Times of all Related Events)
5. WHY   (The Motivation for Actions Taken)
6. HOW   (Details of the Execution Methods)

Locard's Principle of Exchange

The Principle of Exchange—developed by Dr. Edmond Locard (1877-1966), a pioneer in forensic science—states that, "*When a person or object comes into contact with another person or object, a cross-transfer of materials occurs.*" It applies to fragmentary and/or trace evidence that can be used to tie criminals to crime scenes.

It applies equally to Network Forensic Teams conducting network surveillance and investigations, as minute changes to the digital environment made by investigators can be discovered by malicious actors and used to undermine their efforts.

Incident Scene Management

Incident scene management, and evidence management as a part of that, must be learned and incorporated into the investigators' toolkit. The best practices listed below have been developed so First Responders can have the highest probability of a successful outcome when investigations and collected evidence must be defended in a legal environment.

1. Approach and Secure the Incident Scene
2. Survey to Determine Scene Boundaries
3. Evaluate any Physical Evidence Possibilities
4. Take Preliminary Photographs and/or Video
5. Conduct a Detailed Search of the Scene
6. Collect and Record all Evidence Types
7. Conduct a Final Survey and Release the Scene

Field Investigation Toolkits

Regardless of the type of investigation being conducted—physical or digital—standard items should be a part of the Network Forensic Teams' investigative toolkit. The basic items listed below should always be available to the team responding to the incident location.

1. Consent and Authorization Forms
2. Digital Cameras, Extra Memory, and Batteries
3. Notebooks, Pens, and Markers
4. Evidence Collection Containers
5. Evidence Labels, Identifiers, and Seals
6. Photographic Rulers (ABFO Scales)
7. Personal Protective Equipment

Evidence Dynamics

Evidence Dynamics refers to any influence that changes, obscures, adds, contaminates, or obliterate evidences regardless of intent. Understanding the behavior and context of the evidence plays an important role in incident reconstruction. Although originally intended for physically evidence it is equally applicable to digital evidence and artifacts.

For example, evidence dynamics can be used to describe the behavior of execution mechanisms and the processes implemented during the actual incident.

Chain of Custody (Part I)

Chain of Custody refers to the documentation of acquisition, control, analysis, and disposition of physical and digital evidence. This documentation will contain the following information:

1. The Person Handling the Evidence
2. Any Processes and Procedures Performed
3. The Time and Date of Evidence Acquisition
4. The Original Location of any Collected Evidence
5. The Methods of Evidence Collection
6. The Methods of Examination and Analysis
7. The Reason for the Evidence Collection

Chain of Custody (Part II)

Intentional (tampering) or unintentional (accidental) changes to digital and physical evidence presents risks in any investigation. The items below are subject to Chain of Custody practices.

1. Photographs
2. Reports
3. Lab Information
4. Notebooks

5. Checklists
6. Log Files
7. Videos and Screen Captures

Investigative Interview Strategies

In most investigations, interviews are the main tool investigators use to find out what happened and/or verify physical and technical evidence. A good investigation interview is only as good as the person conducting it, regardless of the nature of the investigation itself. The best practices listed below help to ensure successful outcomes when conducting investigative interviews.

1. Create a Comprehensive Question List
2. Select a Non-Threatening Location
3. Maintain an Open and Objective Mind
4. Ask Open-Ended Questions
5. Start with the Easy Questions
6. Keep Your Opinions to Yourself
7. Focus Solely on the Facts
8. Ask about Additional Witnesses
9. Ask about Additional Evidence
10. Do not Retaliate Against the Interviewee
11. Request Further Contact for More Information
12. Keep the Interview Confidential
13. Document and/or Record all Interviews

Nonverbal Communication

We respond daily to thousands of nonverbal cues and behaviors including postures, facial expression, eye gaze, gestures, and tone of voice. Listed below are several nonverbal cues with which investigators should be familiar.

1. Facial Expressions and Eye Contact
2. Body Movements, Posture, and Hand Gestures

3. Paralanguage and Incongruent Communication
4. Physiological and Emotional Changes

Documenting Interviews

Preparation is essential when interviewing and documenting potential targets and witnesses during any investigation.

1. Prepare a List of Interview Questions
2. Leave Ample Space Between Questions
3. Divide the Notation Space into Two Sections
4. Balance Note-Taking and Active Listening
5. Limit Notes to the Most Important Phrases
6. Devise Your Own Efficient Note-Taking System
7. Notate any Answers Requiring a Follow-Up

[This page intentionally left blank]

DOMAIN 06

Investigative Principles and Lead Development

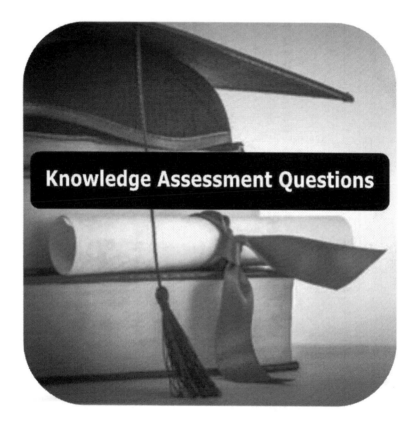

The following knowledge assessment questions are presented in true / false, multiple choice, and fill-in-the-blank formats. The correct answers are provided in an Answer Key at the end of this text. These questions may or may not be presented on the actual certification exam.

Domain 06: Knowledge Assessment Questions

Which choice below refers to any influence that changes, obscures, adds, contaminates, or obliterates evidence regardless of intent?

A. Evidence Dynamics

B. Chain of Custody

C. Scene Management

D. Evidence Management

E. None of the Above

_____ define(s) the elements of a claim and are typically driven by the primary consumer of the investigative report.

A. Chain of Custody

B. Probable Cause

C. Elements of Proof

D. Reasonable Doubt

E. None of the Above

Which choice below is the first action an Incident Response Team investigator should take when documenting any interview?

A. Balance Notes and Active Listening

B. Limit Notes to the Most Important Phrases

C. Prepare a List of Interview Questions

D. Notate Answers Requiring Follow-Up

E. None of the Above

The non-verbal cue referred to as _____ can be defined as, "*A pattern in which the sender gives conflicting messages on verbal and nonverbal levels.*"

A. Paralinguistic Communication

B. Incongruent Communication

C. Haptic Communication

D. Proxemic Communication

E. None of the Above

Which choice below refers to the documentation of acquisition, control, analysis, and disposition of physical and digital evidence?

A. Evidence Dynamics

B. Chain of Custody

C. Scene Management

D. Evidence Management

E. None of the Above

A(n) _____ is a systematic inquiry and/or examination, typically conducted for the purpose of identifying and/or verifying facts.

A. Negotiation

B. Consultation

C. Interrogation

D. Investigation

E. None of the Above

Which choice below is the first action an Incident Response Team investigator should take when managing an incident scene?

A. Survey to Determine the Scene Boundaries

B. Evaluate the Physical Evidence Possibilities

C. Conduct a Detailed Search of the Scene

D. Approach and Secure the Incident Scene

E. None of the Above

_____ states, "*When a person or object comes into contact with another person or object, a cross-transfer of materials occurs.*"

A. Locard's Principle of Exchange

B. Cultural Transmission Theory

C. Symbolic Interaction Theory

D. Social Construction Theory

E. None of the Above

Domain 06: *Investigative Principles and Lead Development*

What choice below best represents the primary purpose and importance of evidence dynamics in incident response investigations?

A. Mitigation of the Incident

B. Remediation of the Incident

C. Reconstruction of the Incident

D. Eradication of the Incident

E. None of the Above

Regardless of the type of investigation being conducted—physical or digital—_____ items should be a part of the investigative toolkit.

A. Operational

B. Technical

C. Standard

D. Personal

E. None of the Above

What choice below is **not** a best practice for investigators when conducting and documenting any type of interview?

A. Select a Non-Threatening Location

B. Ask "Yes" and "No" Questions

C. Ask about Apparent Contradictions

D. Keep the Interview Confidential

E. None of the Above

The non-verbal cue referred to as _____ can be defined as, *"The non-lexical component of communication such as intonation, pitch and speed of speaking."*

A. Paralanguage

B. Incongruence

C. Haptics

D. Proxemics

E. None of the Above

Domain 06: *Investigative Principles and Lead Development*

All case types and investigations have the same considerations—whether the goal is litigation or developing a stronger security posture.

1. True

2. False

Regardless of the type of investigation being conducted—physical or digital—standard items should be a part of the investigative toolkit.

1. True

2. False

Evidence Dynamics refers to any influence that changes, obscures, adds, contaminates, or obliterates networks or systems regardless of intent.

1. True

2. False

In most investigations, interviews are the primary tool investigators use to find out what happened and/or verify physical and technical evidence.

1. True

2. False

We respond to thousands of verbal cues and behaviors including postures, facial expression, eye gaze, gestures, and tone of voice.

1. True

2. False

Preparation is the key to so many endeavors in life and interviewing potential targets and witnesses during investigations is no exception.

1. True

2. False

DOMAIN 07

Investigation Planning and Preparation

Defining the Network Forensic Mission

In a quote offered by strategist Mark Caine, *"Meticulous planning will enable everything a person does to appear spontaneous."* While every event during a network incident cannot be predicted, defining the Network Forensic Teams' mission will keep the team members focused and set realistic expectations within the organization.

Additionally, it is critical that all elements of the network forensic mission be completely supported and endorsed by senior leadership to be successful. Listed below are 12 prominent areas to be considered when defining the mission of the team and the role of individual members participating in the forensic investigation during an incident response.

1. **Respond with an Organized Process**: In the initial chaos and confusion inherent to all network incidents, a measured and calculated response will be required. No two incidents are alike, but each share commonalities that allow for the development of organized response processes.

2. **Complete and Impartial Investigation**: The goal of network forensic investigators participating in an incident is to use their skills to gather facts, turn facts into actionable leads, and turn leads into solutions facilitating remediation. Opinions and theories will always be present, but it will be facts that ensure a complete and impartial investigation is conducted by the team.

3. **Quickly Confirm / Deny the Incident**: On occasion, a perceived incident may prove to be a false alarm that must be dismissed quickly for financial, reputational, and operational reasons. On other occasions, incidents prove to be real and must be dealt with efficiently and effectively. The teams' ability to quickly confirm or deny an incident requires a fine balance between unnecessarily "crying wolf" and suffering from "paralysis by analysis."

4. **Assess Damage and Scope**: Once the team determines an incident has occurred, assessing the damage and scope

quickly is a critical requirement. The team must know and understand the policies, procedures, and resources it has at its disposal and utilize them properly.

5. **Control and Contain Incident**: Once the scope of an incident is known and a damage assessment has been conducted, the incident must be controlled and contained. The methodology will vary based on numerous factors such as severity, available resources, and the context in which the incident occurred.

6. **Collect and Document Evidence**: The primary mission of a network forensic investigator involved in any incident is to collect and document evidence which may be used at a later time in legal actions. When defining the mission and roles within the team, ensure the proper tools, training, and resources exist to support a successful outcome.

7. **Select Additional Resources**: The time to discover the Incident Response Team requires additional resources is not in the midst of an ongoing incident. The decision to secure additional resources – such as outsourced Incident Response personnel, legal counsel, or vendor support – must be considered when the Incident Response mission is initially defined.

8. **Protect Established Privacy Rights**: Even during armed conflicts between nations, the Geneva Convention demands standards such as the *Humanitarian Law of Armed Conflicts* are followed. Incident Response personnel must adhere to official policies and procedures establishing privacy rights of third-parties and peripheral actors are protected with all reasonable efforts.

9. **Provide an Effective Liaison**: An Incident Response Team is interdisciplinary by nature and communicates with a wide variety of technical and non-technical personnel. Choose an effective liaison to communicate with ancillary personnel to ensure messaging is consistent and nothing "gets lost in the translation."

10. **Maintain Appropriate Confidentiality**: The need for security and confidentiality may appear to be self-evident but can be unknowingly and unintentionally violated by Incident Response Teams. A genuine "need to know," not a persons' title, must be the standard measure of access.

11. **Provide Expert Testimony**: One of the responsibilities of forensic investigators is to provide expert testimony in a court of law when summoned to do so. When defining the role and responsibilities of the Incident Response Team take this into account by creating standardized documents, formatted reports, and mandatory procedures for taking case notes.

12. **Recommendations Supported by Facts**: The Incident Response life cycle dictates "strategic recommendations" be made as part of any post-incident remediation effort. As with any expert opinion put forward in an official report, ensure any strategic recommendations are supported by facts included in formal reports. Expert recommendations and opinions which are supported by well-sourced facts are typically easy to defend.

Internal Communication Procedures

The threat of malicious actors watching forensic investigators while the investigators watch them during an Incident Response is neither theoretical nor hypothetical. Team members can increase the security of their internal communications by following a few common-sense guidelines.

1. Encrypt ALL Email
2. Properly Label ALL Documents
3. Properly Label ALL Communications
4. Monitor Conference Call Participation
5. Use Case Numbers and/or Project Names

External Communication Procedures

It is likely that an Incident Response Team will need to determine a standard methodology for communicating with third-parties such as vendors, partners, or law enforcement. It is also advisable to use approved and established channels, such as Public Relations or Legal Counsel, to avoid unintentional disclosures.

When establishing policies and procedures for communicating with personnel external to the team, consider the following questions for determining the best methods of maintaining an appropriate level of communication.

1. Does the Incident Meet a Reporting Threshold?
2. Reporting for Incident Detection or Confirmation?
3. How are Third-Parties Notified?
4. Do Existing Contracts Protect Confidentiality?
5. Who is Responsible for Disclosure?
6. How Does Disclosure Occur?
7. Are There Penalties Resulting from Disclosure?
8. Does the Timing of Disclosure Impact Penalties?
9. Are Investigative Restraints Expected?
10. Will Third-Parties Participate in the Process?
11. Does Disclosure Impact Remediation?
12. Are There Short-, Medium-, or Long-Term Impacts?

Forensic Team Deliverables

Forensic investigative teams should explicitly define primary deliverables such as formal reports and case notes, including a realistic target completion time and recurrence intervals. Examples of common deliverables and their associated time frames are listed below.

1. Case Status Report   (Daily)
2. Live Response Report   (Two Days)
3. Malware Analysis Report   (Five Days)
4. Forensic Report   (Six Days)

5. Intrusion Investigation Report   (Eight Days)

Building a Field Forensic System

The majority of incidents involving networks will require investigators to perform forensic work outside of a controlled lab environment. Although the chosen system will be unique to the needs and composition of the Incident Response Team, there are a number of common factors that should be considered.

1. Memory   (Maximum Capacity)
2. CPU   (Top Tier)
3. I/O Buses   (High-Speed Interfaces)
4. Laptops   (Screen Size and Resolution)
5. Portability   (Weight Matters)
6. Warranty Service   (2=1, 1=0)
7. Internal Storage   (Large and Encrypted)

Building a Forensic Field Kit

Incident Response Team members, and especially network forensic investigators, use a set of shared resources in addition to those for daily use at their assigned workstations. Teams should keep a pool of specialized hardware at their office and make it available for checkout as needed.

Although the chosen equipment will be unique to the needs and composition of the Incident Response Team, there are a number of common items that should be considered.

1. Duplication and Imaging Systems
2. Write Blockers for all Interface Types
3. Mobile Device Acquisition Systems
4. Assorted Cables and Adapters
5. Large External Hard Drives
6. Blank CD's and DVD's
7. Network Switches and Cabling

8. Power Strips and Electrical Cables
9. I/O Bus Cables (eSATA, USB, Firewire)
10. Interfaces (PATA, SATA, SCSI, SAS)
11. Computer Maintenance Tools

Case Studies: Admissibility of Forensic Evidence

Daubert v. Merrell, 509 US 579 (1993)
Shifted focus from a test for general acceptance
to a test for reliability and relevance.

Kumbo Tire Co et al. v. Carmichael et al (1993)
Tests set forth in *Daubert* standard were insufficient
for testing cases where methodology was not
formed on a scientific framework.

Admissibility of Forensic Evidence: *Daubert*

There is no strict definition for "forensically sound": a judge will decide the admissibility of evidence on a case-by-case basis. In the case of *Daubert v. Merrell (1993)* the court addressed the issue of "Reliability and Relevance" of forensic techniques based on the questions listed below.

1. Is the Technique Empirically Tested?
2. Is the Technique Subject to Peer Review?
3. Is There a Known Potential Error Rate?
4. Do Standards Control the Operation?
5. Is There Acceptance by the Scientific Community?

Admissibility of Forensic Evidence: *Kumbo*

The *Daubert* method was no less valid, but the law had not yet been provisioned to account for this type of analysis. In the case of *Kumbo v. Carmichael (1993)* the court not only further addressed the issue of "Reliability and Relevance" of forensic techniques, but of the expert witness as well based on the questions listed below.

1. Is the Technique Utilized Beyond Litigation?
2. Is Evidence Based on Qualitatively Sufficient Data?
3. Is There a Consistency of Process and Methods?
4. Does the Expert Possesses Adequate Credentials?
5. Does the Technique Differ from Similar Approaches?
6. Is the Technique Represented in Literature?

Forensic Team Software

The software utilized by forensic investigators will be unique to the needs of the team, but there are commonalities that should be considered for all circumstances. Additionally, the software will be required for more than acquisition; creation of IOC's, log analysis, and reporting should be considered as well. Several considerations are listed below.

1. Boot Disks   (Backtrack, Helix, CAINE)
2. Operating Systems
3. Virtual Machine Platforms
4. Disk Imaging Tools
5. Memory Capture and Analysis
6. Live Response Capture and Analysis
7. IOC Creation and Search Utilities
8. Forensic Examination Suites
9. Log Analysis   (Static, Dynamic)
10. Analysis and Reporting   (Graphics, Charts)

Preparing the Infrastructure: Device Configuration

Prior to performing any incident or forensic investigation, the team should have the ability to search for relevant material and to easily acquire data across the enterprise.

Domain 07: *Investigation Planning and Preparation*

When collecting data on computing device configuration that may be of interest, consider incorporating the best practices listed below.

1. Asset Management
2. Performing Surveys
3. Documenting Instrumentation
4. Planning Steps to Improve Security

Preparing the Infrastructure: Network Configuration

Good information security practices and change management policies promote rapid incident response and enhances the remediation process. When collecting data on network configuration of interest prior to initiating an investigation, consider collecting facts on the following areas listed below.

1. Network Segmentation and Architecture
2. Access Control and Identity Management
3. Instrumentation Documentation
4. Network Services and Applications

Asset Management Surveys

Organizations have different categories of information about network resources and systems in different places; at times this information is geographically dispersed. It is imperative for teams to understand how to access this data when it is needed for an investigation.

Conducting asset management surveys will provide Network Forensic Teams with the following information about each network asset.

1. Date Provisioned
2. Ownership
3. Business Unit
4. Physical Location

5. Contact Information
6. Role or Services
7. Network Configuration

Network Resource Surveys

An organizations' standard system build, software inventories, and other documentation will rarely provide the entire IT infrastructure picture. Forensic investigators should conduct network resource surveys prior to any investigation to determine the information listed below.

1. Operating Systems
2. Hardware
3. Networking Technologies
4. Security Software
5. IT Management Software
6. Endpoint Applications
7. Business and System Applications

Network Resource Logs

Network Forensic Teams have a critical dependency on network resource logs and the information they contain. Examine each process and service within the environment to better understand where logging is retained and how it is controlled. A number of common network log sources are listed below.

1. Web Servers
2. Proxy Servers
3. Firewall, IDS, IPS, and AV
4. Databases
5. Email, Chat, and VoIP
6. DHCP Lease Assignments
7. Custom and Proprietary Applications

IDS, IPS, and Antivirus (AV) Log Challenges

Defensive applications such as antivirus software should be configured to help investigations, not hinder them, and control of their solutions should be retained. If antivirus solutions are not configured to support investigations by quarantining threats, they may transmit the malware by default to the vendor.

In addition to causing the vendor to implement updates too soon and impede the investigation, the transmitted malware may contain sensitive information – such as credentials and proxy settings – the victim organization does not want released. A number of consequences which may also impede an investigation are listed below.

1. Deleting Malware Upon Detection
2. Cannot Analyze IOC's, IP's, or Malware
3. Loss of Targeted Malware Information
4. Investigators Cannot Analyze the Nature of the Attack

10 Steps to Help Reduce Incidents

Many network incidents are the result of procedures and policies which do not represent industry best practices. In many cases, the damage suffered by a victim organization is a self-inflicted wound.

The 10 steps listed below are effective actions that can be taken during the investigation of an ongoing incident – such as posturing and containment actions – but will also provide value as "remediation suggestions" in a final report as well.

The ability of the Incident Response Team to apply these best practices will be contingent on the incidents' severity, context, environment, and the willingness of senior leadership to support the actions.

1. Implement an Operating System Patch Solution
2. Implement an Application Patch Solution
3. Restrict Local Administrator Access if Possible
4. Implement Correct Firewall and AV Configuration

5. Decommission End-of-Life Systems
6. Implement a Configuration Management System
7. Enforce Application and Services Whitelisting
8. Implement Two-Factor Authentication Protocols
9. Conform to DISA STIG's and NSA Cybersecurity Standards
10. Require Two Accounts (and 2F) for Administrators

DISA: Defense Information Systems Agency

The Defense Information Systems Agency is a United States Department of Defense combat support agency composed of military, federal civilians, and contractors.

STIG: Security Technical Implementation Guide

A Security Technical Implementation Guide is a cybersecurity methodology for standardizing security protocols within networks, servers, computers, and logical designs to enhance overall security.

NSA: National Security Agency

The National Security Agency is a national-level intelligence agency of the United States Department of Defense, under the authority of the Director of National Intelligence. The Information Assurance Directorate of the NSA has now been changed to NSA Cybersecurity as of 01 October 2018.

[This page intentionally left blank]

DOMAIN 07

Investigation Planning and Preparation

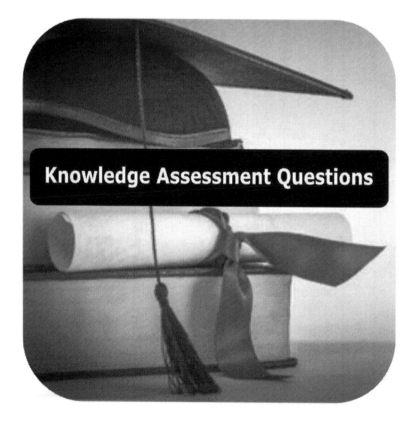

The following knowledge assessment questions are presented in true / false, multiple choice, and fill-in-the-blank formats. The correct answers are provided in an Answer Key at the end of this text. These questions may or may not be presented on the actual certification exam.

Domain 07: Knowledge Assessment Questions

When formatting an Incident Response report, forensic investigators can benefit by utilizing formal reporting guidelines, language guidelines, and _____.

A. Peer Review

B. Proof Reading

C. Standard Templates

D. Appropriate Charts and/or Graphs

E. None of the Above

Which best practice for external communication should a forensic investigator utilize when involved in any type of incident response?

A. Properly Label ALL Communications

B. Monitor Conference Call Participation

C. Properly Label ALL Documents

D. Encrypt ALL Email

E. All of the Above

When defining the Incident Response mission, the ability to _____ is **not** a critical goal of the forensic investigator.

A. Respond with and Organized Process

B. Quickly Confirm or Deny the Incident

C. Assess the Damage and Scope

D. Allocate Financial Resources

E. None of the Above

Defining the Incident Response mission in advance will keep the team focused and set realistic goals. Which consideration below does **not** support this initiative?

A. Assess the Damage and Scope

B. Quickly Confirm or Deny the Incident

C. Purchase External Hard Drives

D. Respond with an Organized Process

E. All of the Above

Domain 07: *Investigation Planning and Preparation*

Forensic investigators should place a high level of importance on _____ when selecting the tools needed for Incident Response in field environments.

A. Portability

B. Availability

C. Cost

D. Popularity

E. None of the Above

Daubert v. Merrell (1993) shifted focus from a test for general acceptance to a test for reliability and relevance. Which answer below does **not** apply to the case?

A. Is the Technique Empirically Tested?

B. Is the Technique Subject to Peer Review?

C. Is There a Known Error Rate?

D. Is the Technique Successful in Court?

E. All of the Above

In preparation for conducting forensics in a field environment, investigators should maintain a set of _____ interfaces in their response toolkits.

A. PATA

B. SCATA

C. SCSI

D. SAS Support

E. All of the Above

When conducting an Asset Management Survey, which of the following should be documented by the Incident Response Team?

A. Memory Capture and Analysis Tools

B. Date the Device was Provisioned

C. Access Control and Identity Management

D. Steps Required to Improve Security

E. All of the Above

Forensic investigators involved with Incident Response must plan to take _____ into consideration when preparing to assess computing device configuration on a network infrastructure.

A. Steps to Improve Security

B. Documenting Instrumentation

C. Performing Surveys

D. Asset Management

E. All of the Above

When conducting an Asset Management Survey, which of the following should **not** be documented by the Incident Response Team?

A. IOC Creation and Search Utilities

B. Date the Device was Provisioned

C. Physical Location of the Device

D. Device Role or Service

E. All of the Above

An organizations' _____, software inventories, and other documentation will rarely provide a forensic investigator with the entire IT infrastructure picture.

A. System Administrator

B. Hardware Inventory

C. Standard System Build

D. Information Security Policy

E. None of the Above

When conducting a Network Resource Survey, which of the following should be documented by the Incident Response Team?

A. Operating System Patch Solutions

B. Restricting Local Administrator Access

C. Utilizing Two-Factor Authentication

D. IT Management Software

E. All of the Above

The majority of incidents involving networks will require investigators to perform forensic work outside of their lab environment.

1. True

2. False

Use approved and established channels for all external communications, such as Business Unit managers or Human Resource personnel, to avoid unintentional disclosures.

1. True

2. False

Kumbo Tire Co et al. v. Carmichael et al (1993) shifted the focus from a test for general acceptance to a test for reliability and relevance.

1. True

2. False

There is no strict definition for "forensically sound": a judge will decide the admissibility of evidence on a case-by-case basis.

1. True

2. False

Good human resource practices and sound business management policies promote rapid response and enhance the remediation process.

1. True

2. False

When considering network resource logs, examine each process and service within the environment to better understand where logging is retained and how it is controlled.

1. True

2. False

DOMAIN 08

Forensic Analysis Methodology

General Process for Performing Analysis

As a practitioner in the field of Network Forensics, Incident Response, or Information Security, it is hard to deny the importance of science. Regardless of application, the proven steps listed below for conducting analysis are always based on the Scientific Method.

1. Define and Understand the Objectives
2. Obtain the Relevant Data
3. Inspect the Data Content
4. Perform the Data Conversion and/or Normalization
5. Select an Analysis Method
6. Perform the Analysis
7. Evaluate the Results

Define the Objectives

Making objectives is not difficult but making good objectives that are realistic can be challenging. Defining realistic objectives requires the network forensic investigator to have a solid working knowledge of the technology involved and the situation in which that technology will be applied. Listed below are several questions to be answered when defining objectives.

1. What is the Investigator Trying to Determine?
2. Do Conclusions Exist from Available Facts?
3. How much Time will be Involved?
4. What Investigative Resources are Needed?
5. Who is Interested in the Results?
6. What is a Successful Outcome for the Results?

Know Your Data

Prior to performing an analysis, investigators must explore all the possible sources of data and understand how to use them. The primary task of any network forensic investigation is to perform data collection and use the collected data for analysis. To answer investigative questions effectively the collected data must be useful and relevant to the investigation.

Once the investigator has determined what data sources exist and are available, they will have a better understanding of what data those sources can provide and what data they need to collect.

Where is Data Stored?

In an investigative context, the term "data" is used in a broad sense consisting of four primary categories: operating system files, applications, databases, and user data. Listed below are several common sources of data investigators will encounter in the field.

1. Desktops, Laptops, and Tablets
2. Servers
3. Mobile Devices
4. Storage Solutions and External Media
5. System and Network Devices
6. Cloud Storage Solutions
7. Back-Ups and Data Recovery Media

Available Data Sources

From a general investigative analysis standpoint, four high-level categories of evidence may exist in the seven locations previously stated above. Listed below are the four high-level categories and some examples of data available from those sources.

1. **Operating Systems**: Windows Registry, Unix Syslog, and Mac OS X.

2. **Applications**: Cache, Files, Logs, and Preferences.

3. **User Data**: Centralized Locations, Decentralized Locations, Host-Based, Network-Based.

4. **Network Services and Devices**: Cache, Files, Logs, and Reporting.

Accessing Data Sources

Once an investigator has obtained data to analyze, one of the first challenges they may encounter is figuring out how to access it. One of the most important questions to ask will be, *"Is the data in an accessible state?"* Listed below are several challenges to accessing data investigators may encounter in the field.

1. Data may be Encrypted
2. Data may be Encoded
3. Data may be Compressed
4. Data may be Custom Formatted
5. Data may be on Various Drives and/or Images
6. Data may be Damaged or Destroyed

Disk Images

Investigators must always ask questions regarding the data they receive and get basic answers to those questions to ensure they understand how to handle it. When evidence is provided without proper context, not asking the correct questions will increase the probability of wasted time.

Listed below are several sample questions an investigator would ask when being told they were about to receive a "copy" of a "hard drive" from a "system."

1. What is the Type of Image Format?
2. Is Disk Encryption Utilized?
3. Are Libraries from Administrators Available?
4. O/S (What is the Make, Model, Version, and Function?)
5. RAID (What is the Make, Model, Card, and Settings?)

Domain 08: *Forensic Analysis Methodology*

Outline the Investigative Approach: General

Investigative questions and information may provide valuable leads, but keep in mind they could be partially or completely false. Listed below are seven areas of general interest investigators may find useful for developing valid and factual leads.

1. Network Information Flow Data
2. Network Egress Points
3. Volume of Data Transferred (Benchmark, Actual)
4. Specific Protocols and Ports
5. Network Instrumentation Anomalies
6. Repeated Failed Login Attempts
7. Logs (DNS, Proxy, Firewall, and Router)

Outline the Investigative Approach: Targeted

Once a general investigative approach has been outlined and the research has been conducted, the information gathered can then be applied to a more specific and targeted approach. As with the general approach, the targeted approach should be outlined as well to keep focus on the mission.

Listed below are several areas of interest to an investigator searching for evidence of data theft or data manipulation and understanding these artifacts can potentially reveal an attackers' methodology.

1. Abnormal User Activity
2. Login Activity Outside Expected Hours
3. Odd Connection Durations
4. Unexpected Connection Sources
5. Abnormally High CPU Utilization
6. Compression Tool Artifacts
7. Recently Installed and/or Modified Services

Malware Detection Strategy

It is important for investigators to create a streamlined approach and outline for their malware detection strategy. It is unlikely an investigator would review every combination of bytes or possible locations to store malware on a network or system drive.

Listed below are several elements of a malware detection strategy outlined to generate relevant leads to be followed.

1. Review Auto-Start Programs
2. Verify the Integrity of System Binaries
3. Identify Well-Known Artifacts of Infection
4. Perform a Virus Scan of the System (Using Quarantine)
5. Identify Legitimate Files with Malicious Intent

Selection of Analysis Methods

Several analysis methods are commonly used by network forensic investigators across many different types of operating systems, disk images, log files, and other data. The chosen method will be dictated by specific needs and investigative context. Listed below are several high-level points of consideration when selecting an appropriate analysis method for the investigation.

1. Use of External Resources
2. Use of Manual Inspection
3. Use of Specialized Tools
4. Minimization with Sorting and Filtering
5. Use of Statistical Analysis
6. Use of Keyword Searches
7. Use of File and Record Carving

A Note on Artifacts

Although specific implementation details may change, analysis methods are not tied to any particular technology. Artifacts are typically independent of the operating system being utilized; while they may exist in different locations and following different naming conventions, the same artifact information is typically present in all systems.

Investigators should take this into account when developing their investigative tools, tactics, and processes (TTP's) and understand the same investigative processes can be implemented across multiple systems.

Use of External Resources

Using external resources (or other peoples' work) during the investigation is perfectly acceptable when time and resources are limited. There is no need to "recreate the wheel" each time an incident is investigated.

However, investigators must ensure the external resources incorporate reasonable, proven, and accepted methods. Listed below are several external resources commonly utilized during network forensic investigations.

1. Known File Databases
2. Automated Industry Tools
3. Reputable Knowledge Repositories
4. Co-Workers, Colleagues, and Forums
5. National Software Reference Library (NSRL / NIST)
6. Security Vendor Websites

Use of Specialized Tools

Commercial entities, practitioners, and researchers in forensics have created numerous specialized tools to assist in investigators with network forensic investigations. There is no "right" or "wrong" choice of tools; their selection will be based on the needs and context of the investigation.

Every team should have access to a comprehensive collection of specialized tools as each has functional and practical limitations.

Performing a validation to ensure the tools' functionality in a specific environment will save the investigator time when engaged in the tasks listed below.

1. Data Visualization
2. Artifact Analysis
3. Malware Identification
4. File System Metadata Reporting

Use of Sorting and Filtering

Most structured data, meaning data with a parsable record format, is well suited for sorting and filtering. However, most file metadata are not useful during an investigation.

When considering the volume of metadata which exists in hundreds of thousands of files, it quickly becomes obvious only a small subset of metadata will be relevant to the investigative mission. Listed below are four high-level areas of focus when filtering and sorting data.

1. Focus on Specific Dates
2. Focus on Specific Directories
3. Focus on Specific File Names
4. Focus on Specific Attributes

Use of Statistical Analysis

Statistical analysis is typically used in forensic cases in which investigators do not know exactly what they are looking for or how the information can be found. The visibility of endpoints may be low; there is a suspicion of malicious activity but no facts to verify the suspicion.

Additionally, human (manual) discovery may be difficult or impossible, making an automated process the only viable option. Listed below are several examples of useful statistics whose summaries will be based on varying queries.

1. Uncover Patterns and/or Anomalies
2. Automated Parsing of Fields
3. Geolocation Data Discovery
4. System Indexing

Use of Keyword Searches

The "string" or "keyword" search is a basic analysis method that network forensic investigators have used since the creation of computer forensics. The premise is simple: investigators create keyword lists ("strings") and use those lists to search evidence (digital files).

As simple as the premise may be there are a number of nuances and subtleties of which investigators must be aware. If the investigator does not know how the string is represented in the data being searched, the list may not prove to be useful.

There is also the possibility of encoding or formatting of the data, both of which can defeat search attempts. It is important for investigators to not overlook the value of searching unallocated and slack space, as users cannot control what data may be contained in those areas.

Use of File and Record Carving

The purpose of this method is to search for a unique sequence of bytes that corresponds to the header (the first few bytes) of a file. Investigators will typically encounter standard *headers* (marking the beginning of a file) and *footers* (marking the end of a file) in common formats that are accessible with the proper forensic tools.

Listed below are several benefits provided to the investigator using this methodology during data analysis.

1. Can Identify Specific File-Type Instances
2. Not Affected (or Deceived) by File Extensions
3. Can Identify and Read Active or Deleted Files
4. Can Identify and/or Recover Specific File Types

Domain 08: *Forensic Analysis Methodology*

Evaluating Analysis Results

An important aspect of the analysis process is having the investigator evaluate existing results and to adjust investigative methods accordingly. Evaluation of results is typically the most time consuming and the most frustrating aspect of the process.

Many things can go wrong: analysis can generate false positives and false negatives for apparently no reason. In many cases, the root cause of the issue can be due to a simple mistake such as type-o's in the strings.

Investigators are advised to engage in "sanity checking" by continuously evaluating the analysis against the investigative questions being asked. Also consider that the absence of a "hit" is not proof the data *never* existed; it just may not exist *currently* or in the state originally assumed.

Listed below are seven high-level practices that will assist investigators when evaluating analysis results and assist with "sanity checking."

1. Do not Wait Until the Analysis Concludes
2. Spot-Check the Initial Results
3. Ensure the Relevant Investigative Context
4. Evaluate all Results in that Context
5. Define Problems with the Investigative Approach
6. Change Approaches and Sources as Needed
7. Build Evidence to Support an Investigative Position

[This page intentionally left blank]

DOMAIN 08

Forensic Analysis Methodology

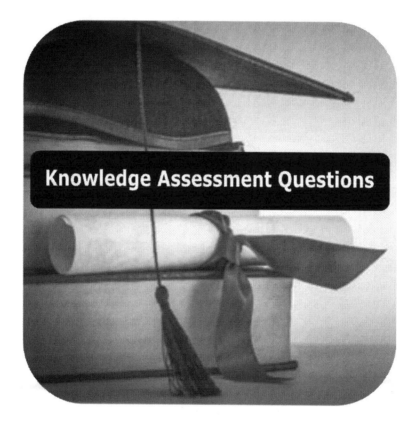

The following knowledge assessment questions are presented in true / false, multiple choice, and fill-in-the-blank formats. The correct answers are provided in an Answer Key at the end of this text. These questions may or may not be presented on the actual certification exam.

Domain 08: Knowledge Assessment Questions

From a general forensic analysis standpoint, various categories of data evidence may be available to an investigator which may include Windows Registry, Unix Syslog, and _____.

A. Operating Systems

B. User Data

C. Applications

D. Network Services and/or Devices

E. All of the Above

Which of the questions listed below is **not** relevant for defining the objectives to be used when performing analysis?

A. How Much Time will be Involved?

B. What Resources are Needed?

C. What Team Members will Participate?

D. What are We Trying to Determine?

E. All of the Above

Once a forensic investigator has obtained data to analyze, one of the first challenges they may encounter is determining how to _____ it.

A. Encrypt

B. Encode

C. Format

D. Access

E. All of the Above

Which of the choices listed below is **not** one of the four high-level categories of data sources available to the network investigator?

A. BYOD Smart Phones and Tablets

B. Operating Systems

C. Applications

D. Network Services and Devices

E. All of the Above

An investigator can search systems for artifacts of data manipulation or theft, and these artifacts can reveal an attackers' _____.

A. Identity

B. Motives

C. Methodology

D. Location

E. All of the Above

Which of the choices listed below is **not** a preferred external resource that can be utilized by network investigators during Incident Response actions?

A. Known File Databases

B. Bulletin Board Systems and/or Social Media

C. Reputable Knowledge Repositories

D. Security Vendor Websites

E. All of the Above

_____ analysis is typically used in cases in which an investigator does not know exactly what they are looking for or how the information can be found.

A. Statistical

B. Prescriptive

C. Diagnostic

D. Descriptive

E. All of the Above

Which of the choices listed below is **not** a characteristic or capability of the analysis technique referred to as "file carving"?

A. Identify Specific File-Type Instances

B. Can Read Active and Deleted Files

C. Can be Affected by File Extensions

D. Analyze Headers in Common Formats

E. All of the Above

Domain 08: *Forensic Analysis Methodology*

When evaluating results during the analysis process, it is important for investigators to identify potential _____ early in the process to avoid misleading conclusions.

A. Third-Party Information

B. Lead Generation

C. Malware Signatures

D. False Positives or Negatives

E. All of the Above

Which of the choice listed below is an action or characteristic associated with evaluating collected data?

A. Many Things can Go Wrong

B. Engage in "Sanity Checking"

C. Do not Wait Until Analysis Concludes

D. Evaluate for Investigative Questions

E. All of the Above

When evaluating and prioritizing analytical results, it is important to consider the _____ to ensure accurate answers to investigative questions.

A. Expert Opinion of Others

B. Relevant Investigative Context

C. Environment of the Incident

D. Scope of the Incident

E. All of the Above

Which of the choices listed below is an example of information sought by forensic investigators when conducting network analysis?

A. Abnormal User Activity

B. Unexpected Connection Sources

C. Abnormally High CPU Utilization

D. Recently Installed and/or Modified Services

E. All of the Above

Domain 08: *Forensic Analysis Methodology*

Investigative questions and information may provide leads, but keep in mind they could be partially or completely false.

1. True
2. False

You can search systems for artifacts of data manipulation or theft, although these artifacts will not reveal an attackers' methodology.

1. True
2. False

Several analysis methods are commonly used across many different types of operating systems, disk images, log files, and other data.

1. True
2. False

When engaged in "file carving," the idea is to search for a common sequence of bytes that corresponds to the body (the first few bytes) of a file.

1. True
2. False

The "string" or "keyword" search is a basic analysis method that digital investigators have used since the creation of computer forensics.

1. True
2. False

Most structured data, meaning data with a parsable record format, is suitable to sort and filter during the investigation and analysis phases of the Incident Response.

1. True
2. False

DOMAIN 09

Principles of
Network Evidence

The Case for Network Monitoring

In some network forensic situations, data captured by a network sensor or other network device is the only evidence actions were taken by an attacker. There are many reasons to monitor a network during an investigation, but seven primary goals typically present themselves on a regular basis.

1. Gather Potentially Actionable Information
2. Turn Intelligence into Signatures
3. Confirm or Dispel Suspicions
4. Accumulate Evidence and Indicators
5. Verify the Scope of the Compromise
6. Identify Additional Parties Involved
7. Generate a Timeline of the Events

Types of Network Monitoring

Network monitoring typically consists of event-based alerts generated by a set of predefined conditions. The tools available to investigators for network monitoring range from free, open-source tools (such as *Snort* or *Suricata*) to enterprise-grade commercial solutions (such as Cisco's *Sourcefire* or RSA *NetWitness*).

In most cases, these NIDS will be placed within a network and be available to investigators for post-processing gathered data. Listed below are four primary levels of detail investigators many choose to gather once network monitoring begins.

1. Header Logging
2. Full Packet Logging
3. Statistical Modeling
4. Data Flow Analysis

Event-Based Alert Monitoring

Event-based alerting is the form of monitoring to which most security and IT personnel are accustomed. Whether using free or commercial platforms, these tools allow the entire enterprise to be monitored easily. Traditional application of this technology is in the form of a Network Intrusion Detection System (NIDS) containing software which monitors network traffic patterns. Events of interest – based on predefined rules and thresholds – trigger alerts that may warrant closer inspection.

Event-based monitoring relies on indicators (or signatures) matched against traffic observed by the network sensor and will typically provide useful information regarding the categories of data listed below. This type of alerting is generated by robust and specific indicators unlikely to return false alerts.

1. Matching on IP / TCP Headers
2. Serial Number Identification
3. Validity Date Identification
4. Issuer Name Identification

Header and Full Packet Logging

In many cases, the decision on how to handle network data depends on the subject(s) being monitored, and for what reason. The means by which the header and packet capture is performed is also affected by the purposes of the investigation. This type of logging can monitor network activity, collect transferred system data, and help the Network Forensic Team generate and/or refine signatures.

Additionally, specialized tools (such as *Wireshark*) can assist in targeted investigations by retaining entire sessions comprised of raw packets which represent actual communication. Listed below are several benefits and common uses for this type of network logging.

1. Collect Transferred System Data
2. Monitor Network Activity
3. Identify Potentially Stolen Data
4. Generate Evidence to Support Legal Matters
5. Locate Evidence to Support Internal Investigations

Domain 09: *Principles of Network Evidence*

Statistical Monitoring

Statistical monitoring focuses on the high-level view of what information flows, or connections, are traversing the network. It is valuable for situations in which investigators have an incomplete visibility of network endpoints, suspect suspicious activity, but have little information to support investigative theories.

This type of monitoring generates data suitable for pattern analysis (using tools such as *NetFlow* or *ARGUS*). These types of data streams contain a count of the number of bytes and packets for each "flow," or session, observed by a device.

Listed below are several data collection capabilities that typically prove useful to network forensic investigators.

1. Capture and Parse Protocol Headers
2. Interpret Timing and Packet Structures
3. Identify Suspected Malicious Communications
4. Detect Unauthorized and/or External Port Scans
5. Detect Characteristics of Beaconing
6. Detect Data Flows in Opposite Directions
7. Answer Specific Investigative Questions

Setting Up a Network Monitoring System

Intrusion Detection System (IDS) platforms cannot reliably perform both intrusion detection and network surveillance duties simultaneously. When IDS is configured for full-content capture its effectiveness as a network sensor diminishes.

Accordingly, any reallocation of IDS resources requires the Network Forensic Team to engage in detailed planning and preparation before deployment. Listed below are several factors investigators must consider that may serve to diminish sensor performance.

1. Affected by Network Architecture
2. Affected by Network Bandwidth

3. Affected by Segment Utilization

4. Affected by Non-Technical Influences

Network Surveillance

When investigators plan to conduct a network surveillance it is best to begin the investigation in "tactical" mode; make no assumption of any benefit derived from long-term monitoring. This approach applies regardless of the tools deployed (such as a SPAN port, hardware network tap, or Snort sensor with TCPDUMP).

Prior to beginning the network monitoring investigators should be aware of several factors listed below that may have a negative impact on the network surveillance mission. A flaw in one (or more) of these steps could produce unreliable and ineffective surveillance capabilities within the organization.

Worse yet, these flaws can lead to unexpected and unintended legal actions brought against those responsible for managing the investigation.

1. **Define Network Surveillance Goals**: Networks tend to be large and geographically dispersed; casting a wide net with the hope of finding specific data does not work well, nor is it time effective. Carefully define the systems of interest and define the investigative mission around those systems.

2. **Ensure Proper Legal Standing**: Investigators must have formal and written permission to engage in surveillance activities within a network. Additionally, consider the fact that leased segments of the network – those not operated by the organization in question – may exist and are beyond the scope of the investigation.

3. **Acquire and Implement Proper Tools**: The proper tool is the one capable of doing the work effectively. It does not matter if the tool is free or commercial, as long as it scales well for enterprise-grade monitoring and investigations.

4. **Ensure Platform Security**: The monitoring platform must be secured in such a way as to prevent access from those not involved with the investigation. A lack of security may call the integrity and validity of the collected data into question and violate the chain of custody as well.

5. **Ensure Appropriate Placement**: Appropriate placement of monitoring devices ensures the highest probability of a successful investigative outcome. An investigator tracking sensitive information being exfiltrated from a network must not overlook egress points.

6. **Evaluate Captured Data Against Goals**: If the captured data does not support the investigative mission, reevaluate the sensor signatures and/or the defined mission. Monitoring processes are iterative and subject to change.

Network Sensor Deployment: Considerations

The placement of the network sensor is possibly the most important factor and investigator must consider when setting up a monitoring system. An understanding of the network is essential to the success of the investigation.

Listed below are questions an investigator must consider prior to the deployment of a network sensor device.

1. Is the Location of Network Egress Points Known?
2. Are there Specific Routes for Internal Traffic?
3. Are there Specific Routes for External Traffic?
4. Does the Network have any "Choke Points"?
5. Are the Network Boundary Locations Known?
6. How is Endpoint Traffic Encapsulated?
7. Are NAT Devices and/or Web Proxies in Use?

Network Sensor Deployment: Best Practices

The configuration and security of the network sensor are relevant to the potential evidence it may capture. Investigators must take into consideration the points listed below if they intend to maintain the integrity of the investigative data collected.

1. The Sensor is Placed in Physically Secure Location
2. The Chain of Custody Defines Investigative Control
3. Protect the Sensor from Unauthorized Access
4. Ensure the Patch Management System is Updated
5. Document Everything at all Times

Network Monitor Evaluation

Poorly written signatures (including type-o's in IOC's) can cause the software to drop packets simply because the signature engine cannot keep up with the data flow. The data gathered from any network monitoring and/or surveillance must be continually assessed and evaluated to ensure the intended outcome of the collection process.

Listed below are six actions investigators may undertake to ensure the highest probability of a successful mission outcome.

1. Verify the Operation of all Sensors
2. Test Signatures to Generate Sample Alerts
3. Closely Monitor the Statistics
4. Log the Performance Metrics
5. Check Relevant Drivers and Hardware
6. Verify the Data Volume and Packet Arrival Rate

Collecting Network Event Logs

Network events logs have the potential to provide investigators with a wealth of information – if they know the capability of the logging systems and where those systems reside. Listed below are six examples of common network logging sources and the potential information those sources may yield to investigators.

Example #01:

Routers, firewalls, servers, IDS sensors, and other network devices may maintain logs recording network-based events.

Example #02:

DHCP servers log network access when a system requests a specific address.

Example #03:

Firewalls allow system administrators an extensive amount of granularity when creating audit logs.

Example #04:

IDS sensors may catch a portion of an attack due to a signature recognition or anomaly detection filter.

Example #05:

Host-based sensors may detect the alteration of a system library, or the addition of files in sensitive locations.

Example #06:

System log files from the primary domain controller may show failed authentication during login attempts.

Network Logging Challenges

All sources of network-based information can provide investigative clues but often present unique challenges for the network forensic investigator. None of the challenges encountered are so difficult they cannot be overcome.

However, investigators must anticipate these challenges in advance and stand ready to mitigate them with proper planning and preparation.

1. **Data is Stored in Many Formats**: In any given enterprise environment data may be stored in a variety of formats,

contingent upon the needs of the organization. This holds especially true for proprietary formats. Investigators must ask the right questions prior to the investigation and then determine how to best negotiate this challenge.

2. **Data from Several Different O/S's**: During the course of any investigation, multiple operating systems will likely be encountered. This can be especially challenging with both legacy and specialized systems. Asking the right questions will facilitate the compiling of proper field kits to address this challenge at the organizations' location.

3. **Special Software to Access and Read**: Specialized and proprietary software may pose unique analysis issues for investigators in the field. This challenge can be addressed by asking the right questions on an Asset Management Survey and ensuring the forensic suites intended to be used have the capability to interface with these software types.

4. **Network is Geographically Dispersed**: While accessing a network remotely is not desirable some circumstances, it may be unavoidable if a network is distributed over a wide area (or globally). Additionally, laws governing compliance and regulations may change drastically when crossing any national boundaries.

   Investigators will be well-served to utilize the legal and managerial resources of organizations to overcome these challenges

5. **Utilize Inaccurate Time Stamps**: Many systems within a network, operating across many time zones, may have the potential to generate inaccurate time stamps. This can be a challenge when attempting to construct attack timelines. Recognizing this potential and utilizing a single time format for team documentation can mitigate this challenge.

6. **Locating and Correlating all Logs**: A fundamental skill of network investigators is knowing where data resides and then knowing how to access it. Once accessed, it is a very

time-consuming process to correlate log data from varied and dispersed systems. Plan for this challenge accordingly.

7. **Time Consuming and Resource Intensive**: While many investigative teams recognize how time consuming and resource intensive their actions may be, organizations may not share this level of awareness. This holds especially true when key organizational personnel are redirected from their primary functions to assist in network investigations.

   Be prepared to educate senior leadership regarding this reality in advance of starting any investigation.

8. **Maintaining Chain of Custody**: The chain of custody for all collected evidence must be maintained at all times, even over geographically dispersed locations. Create transport and shipping methods for evidence that maintains the chain of custody and minimizes potential loss of integrity.

9. **Reconstructing Network Events**: Developing timelines and reconstructing events is a challenging endeavor that consumes a significant amount of time. This is especially true for networks that maintain logs for short periods of time. Proper planning, experienced insight, and intuition can lessen the impacts of this inevitable challenge.

10. **No Guarantee All Questions Answered**: No matter how experienced the Incident Response Team may be, not every investigative question will yield an answer. While that may be frustrating, it is a reality that must be accepted and planned for in advance of the investigation.

[This page intentionally left blank]

DOMAIN 09

Principles of
Network Evidence

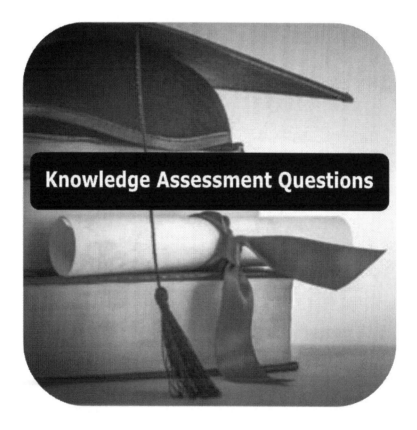

The following knowledge assessment questions are presented in true / false, multiple choice, and fill-in-the-blank formats. The correct answers are provided in an Answer Key at the end of this text. These questions may or may not be presented on the actual certification exam.

Domain 09: Knowledge Assessment Questions

Event-based monitoring relies on indicators (or _____) matched against traffic observed by the network sensor.

A. Flags

B. Signatures

C. Signals

D. Receivers

E. None of the Above

Which of the options listed below does is **not** a viable outcome when making the case for network monitoring?

A. Turn Intelligence into Signatures

B. Accumulate Evidence and Indicators

C. Verify the Scope of the Compromise

D. Identify all Parties Involved

E. All of the Above

Statistical monitoring focuses on the high-level view of what _____, or connections, are traversing the network.

A. Wireless Signals

B. Network Devices

C. Security Alerts

D. Information Flows

E. All of the Above

Which of the statements listed below is **not** a characteristic or capability of event-based alerting in network environments?

A. Free and Commercial Platforms

B. Monitor the Entire Enterprise Easily

C. Any Network Event Triggers Alerts

D. Traditionally Generated by NIDS

E. All of the Above

Intrusion Detection System platforms cannot reliably perform both intrusion detection and _____ duties simultaneously.

A. High-Level Logging

B. Network Surveillance

C. Granular Logging

D. Security Alerts

E. All of the Above

Which of the statements listed below is not a condition in which network investigators would utilize statistical monitoring?

A. Ongoing Activity with Little Information

B. Complete Visibility of the Endpoints

C. Detect Characteristics of Beaconing

D. Used to Answer Specific Questions

E. All of the Above

Poorly written signatures can cause the network monitoring software to drop packets simply because they _____ cannot keep up with the data flow.

A. Wireless Access Point

B. IT Staff

C. Network Cables

D. Signature Engine

E. None of the Above

Which of the questions listed below is a consideration for forensic investigators planning a network sensor deployment?

A. Location of Network Egress Points?

B. Specific Routes for Internal Traffic?

C. "Choke Point" and Boundary Locations?

D. NAT Devices and/or Web Proxies in Use?

E. All of the Above

In some situations, data captured by a(n) _____ or network device is the only evidence that actions were taken by an attacker.
A. System Administrator
B. Third-Party
C. Network Sensor
D. Endpoint User
E. All of the Above

Which of the steps listed below is **not** a required action for implementing and maintaining a network surveillance program?
A. Evaluate Captured Data Against Goals
B. Ensure Appropriate Sensor Placement
C. Consider Platform Security when Feasible
D. Ensure Proper Legal Standing
E. All of the Above

The configuration and security of the network sensor are relevant to the potential _____ it may capture.
A. Signals
B. Packet Headers
C. Evidence
D. Encrypted Traffic
E. All of the Above

Which statement listed below is **not** a potential network logging challenge encountered by forensic investigators attempting to gather and analyze data?
A. Utilization of Inaccurate Time Stamps
B. Log Data is Stored in Similar Formats
C. Requires Special Software to Access and Read
D. Log Data is Geographically Dispersed
E. All of the Above

Domain 09: *Principles of Network Evidence*

Event-based monitoring relies on indicators (or signatures) matched against traffic observed by the network sensor.
1. True
2. False

Statistical monitoring focuses on the low-level view of what network devices, such as Intrusion Detection Systems (IDS), are located on the network.
1. True
2. False

The means by which the header and packet capture is performed is also affected by the purposes of the investigation.
1. True
2. False

Firewalls only allow system administrators an extensive amount of high-level data flow information when creating audit logs.
1. True
2. False

Poorly written signatures can cause the software to drop packets simply because the signature engine cannot keep up with the data flow.
1. True
2. False

Host-based sensors cannot detect the alteration of a system library, or the addition of files in sensitive locations.
1. True
2. False

DOMAIN 10

Initiating Network Forensic Investigations

Time Zones and Investigative Timelines

Accurate timelines are critical for network investigations but tend to pose unforeseen challenges for Incident Response Teams. Timelines are necessary to correlate seemingly events in locations that may be geographically dispersed.

Most systems log events in local time and can be misleading when collected information is assembled from varying time zones.

That reality is further compounded when investigators are faced with Daylight Savings Time. An industry best practice includes the selection of one time standard for the entire team – preferably Coordinated Universal Time (UTC) – that will be used for correlating events and formal reporting requirements.

Using a single time zone like UTC may seem difficult at first, but once established, can benefit Incident Response investigations in numerous ways over the long-term.

Collecting Initial Facts

When interdisciplinary teams are assembled to collect facts about one event, an important consideration is consistency in the type of information gathered by the investigators. Templates and checklists created prior to the incident will facilitate consistency and easy in the initial fact gathering process.

Investigative checklists are not meant to be all-inclusive but are typically common and useful as a starting point for network forensic investigations. Five commonly used checklists are listed below.

1. Incident Summary Checklist
2. Incident Detection Checklist
3. System Details Checklist
4. Network Details Checklist
5. Malware Details Checklist

Incident Summary Checklist

The Incident Summary Checklist provides high-level incident information, a general sense of what happened, and helps identify areas where response protocols might need attention. Once an Incident Summary Checklist has been completed, the investigative team can begin to collect specific details about specific areas.

Several categories of information typically included in an Incident Summary Checklist are provided as examples below.

1. Date and Time the Incident was Reported
2. Date and Time the Incident was Detected
3. Contact Information of the Incident Documenter
4. Contact Information of the Incident Reporter
5. Contact Information of the Incident Detector
6. Nature and Category of the Incident
7. Types of Affected Resources
8. How the Incident was Detected
9. Unique Identifiers of the Affected Resources
10. Access to Systems Since Detection (Personnel)
11. Personnel Aware of the Incident
12. Incident Status (Ongoing, Resolved)
13. Incident Confidentiality Requirements

Incident Detection Checklist

An Incident Detection Checklist is utilized to gather additional specific details regarding how the incident was detected and the mechanisms responsible for the detection themselves. Taking extra time to validate the details of the detection is time well spent for the Incident Response and Forensic Investigative Teams.

Several categories of information typically included in an Incident Detection Checklist are provided as examples below.

1. Automated or Manual Detection
2. Initial Detection Detail Information

3. Contributing Data Sources for the Detection
4. Source Data is Validated and Accurate
5. Source Data is Preserved and Protected
6. Detection Sources' Length of Operation
7. Established Detection Error Rates
8. Any and all Changes to the Data Sources
9. Actual Detection Source (Internal, External)
10. Time Stamps of the Detection Data

System Details Checklist

If the detection details prove to be accurate and consistent, the Incident Response Team must collect system-specific details related to the unique elements of detection. When creating System Details Checklists, avoid grouping systems into single documents; it is easy to overlook details and miss specific, relevant questions.

Several categories of information typically included in a System Details Checklist are provided as examples below.

1. Physical Location of the Affected System
2. IT Asset Tag Number
3. Make and Model of the System
4. Type of Installed Operating System
5. Primary Function of the System
6. Administrator Responsible for the System
7. Assigned IP Addresses (If Applicable)
8. System Host Name and Domain
9. Critical Information on the System
10. Existence of System Back-Ups
11. System is Connected or Disconnected from Network
12. List of all Detected Malware
13. Remediation Steps Already Taken
14. Location of the Preserved System Data

Domain 10: *Initiating Network Forensic Investigations*

Network Details Checklist

Documenting details about the network is important, even in cases where network details do not seem initially important. Several categories of information typically included in a Network Details Checklist are provided as examples below.

1. External Malicious IP Addresses
2. All Domain Names Involved
3. Any Network Monitoring Being Conducted
4. All Remediation Steps Taken
5. All Data Being Preserved
6. All Processes Used to Preserve the Data
7. All Updates to Network Configurations

Malware Details Checklist

The goal of this stage of the investigation is to assemble the facts and circumstances surrounding the discovery of the incident. It is important for members of the Incident Response Team to understand that a significant number of answers to the points in the Malware Details Checklist are not likely to be answered until much later in the investigation (if they can be answered at all).

Several categories of information typically included in a Malware Details Checklist are provided as examples below.

1. Date and Time of the Detection
2. Method of Malware Detection
3. List of the Systems Infected by Malware
4. Name(s) of the Malicious File(s)
5. Name of the Directory Containing the Malware
6. The Family of Malicious File Detected
7. If the Malware is Currently Active
8. If the Malware is Being Preserved
9. The Status of any Malware Analysis
10. If Malware was Submitted to Third-Parties

Maintaining Case Notes

From the moment of initial detection and notification, to the final report and disclosure documents, keeping case notes is critical. Case notes are typically informal documents – but still professional as they may be discoverable – focusing on team activities, not attacker activities. Several purposes and characteristics of case notes are listed below.

1. Keeps the Team Focused
2. Allows Others to Pick Up Team Tasks
3. Allows Third-Parties to Reproduce Efforts
4. Notates Higher-Level Tasks and Results

Building an Attack Timeline

Attack timelines allow network forensic personnel to recreate events and reverse engineer incidents. It is important to realize that events will not necessarily be entered in chronological order (when they were discovered, not when they happened). Listed below are several important factors to consider when building an attack timeline.

1. The Date the Entry was Added
2. The Time of the Event (in UTC)
3. The Host and/or Machine Involved
4. The Event Description (System and Human)
5. Source of the Data (Automated or Human)

Notating entries with this level of detail will help to validate new leads as they arise and assist the network team to keep the effort of the investigation focused on significant activities.

[This page intentionally left blank]

DOMAIN 10

Initiating Network Forensic Investigations

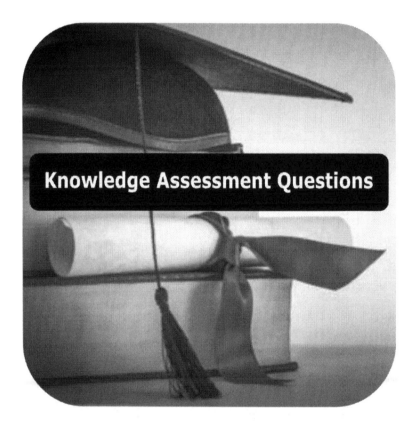

The following knowledge assessment questions are presented in true / false, multiple choice, and fill-in-the-blank formats. The correct answers are provided in an Answer Key at the end of this text. These questions may or may not be presented on the actual certification exam.

Domain 10: Knowledge Assessment Questions

The _____ checklist is not one of the standard forms used by forensic investigators when collecting initial facts during network incidents.

A. System Details

B. Vendor Details

C. Network Details

D. Incident Summary

E. None of the Above

What standardized measure of time are network investigators most likely to use during Incident Response missions?

A. Greenwich Mean Time

B. Coordinated Universal Time

C. Daylight Savings Time

D. Zulu Time Zone

E. All of the Above

When completing an Incident Summary Checklist, the _____ is a critical piece of information for the forensic investigator.

A. Initial Detection Details

B. Detection Error Rates

C. Time of Detection

D. Category of Incident

E. All of the Above

When forensic investigators are collecting initial facts during a network incident, which of the following surveys should **not** be utilized by the Incident Response Team?

A. IT Personnel Checklist

B. Incident Summary Checklist

C. Incident Detection Checklist

D. Network Details Checklist

E. All of the Above

Domain 10: *Initiating Network Forensic Investigations*

When completing an Incident Detection Checklist, the _____
is a critical piece of information for the forensic investigator.

A. Current Incident Status
B. Date and Time of the Incident
C. Contributing Data Source
D. Confidentiality Requirements
E. All of the Above

When completing an Incident Summary Checklist, which of the
following should **not** be documented by the network investigator?

A. Type of Affected Resources
B. Personnel Aware of the Incident
C. Incident Confidentiality Requirements
D. Updates to Network Configurations
E. All of the Above

When completing a System Details Checklist, the _____ is a
critical piece of information for the forensic investigator.

A. IT Asset Tag Number
B. Malicious IP Addresses
C. Network Configuration Updates
D. Family of Malicious Files
E. All of the Above

When completing an Incident Detection Checklist, which of the
following should **not** be documented by the network investigator?

A. Remediation Steps Already Taken
B. Contributing Data Source for Detection
C. Detection Source was Internal and/or External
D. Time Stamps of Detection Data
E. All of the Above

Domain 10: *Initiating Network Forensic Investigations*

When completing a Network Details Checklist, the _____ is a critical piece of information for the forensic investigator.

A. Installed Operating System

B. Assigned IP Addresses

C. Remediation Steps Taken

D. Status of Malware Analysis

E. All of the Above

When completing a System Details Checklist, which of the following should **not** be documented by the network investigator?

A. Physical Location of the Affected System

B. Make and Model of System

C. External Malicious IP Addresses

D. Assigned IP Addresses

E. All of the Above

When completing a Malware Details Checklist, the following are critical pieces of information for the forensic investigator except _____.

A. Method of Detection

B. Personnel Aware of the Incident

C. Family of Malicious File

D. Name of the Malicious File

E. All of the Above

When completing a Network Details Checklist, which of the following should be documented by the network investigator?

A. Method of Malware Detection

B. Process Used to Preserve Data

C. System Still Connected to Network

D. Location of Preserved System Data

E. All of the Above

Domain 10: *Initiating Network Forensic Investigations*

Documenting details about the network is important, even in cases where network details do not seem initially important.

1. True
2. False

Investigators should follow the practice of grouping systems into single documents; consolidating system details makes it easy to reference required information and answer specific, relevant questions.

1. True
2. False

When completing the Malware Details Checklist, the goal of this stage of the investigation is to assemble the facts and circumstances surrounding the discovery of the incident.

1. True
2. False

It is important for investigators to realize that events must be entered in chronological order (when they happened, not when they were discovered).

1. True
2. False

The Incident Summary Checklist is utilized to gather additional details about how incident was detected and the detection system themselves.

1. True
2. False

A large number of answers to the points in the Malware Detection Checklist are not likely to be answered until much later in the investigation (if at all).

1. True
2. False

DOMAIN 11

Initial Development
of Leads

Defining Leads of Value

Sorting the good leads from the bad is important, especially when the organization has a limited team with limited time. In many cases, network forensic investigators will be limited in both areas. Listed below are several steps investigators can take to help ensure the maximization of lead general while utilizing limited resources to accomplish the mission.

1. **The Lead Must Be Relevant**: Some facts may generate leads that prove to be interesting – such as evidence of previous breaches and the presence of malware – but are not relevant to the current investigation. Ensure facts that generate leads to be followed are relevant to the specific and immediate Incident Response mission.

2. **The Lead Must Be Actionable**: Some leads will require unrealistic investigative actions to be pursued, making them less valuable to the investigation. Leads that can be pursued in a reasonable and timely fashion are considered to be actionable and of value to the investigation.

3. **The Lead Must Have Sufficient Detail**: Facts which presented to the Incident Response team with few details cannot be verified as actionable leads. Ensure all gathered leads possess enough detail to formulate a plan of action to pursue them further.

4. **Clarify All Data**: When presented with any information regarding potential leads, make time to clarify all relevant details which generated the lead. Spending adequate time clarifying information on generated leads will potentially save a significant amount of wasted time and resources as the investigation progresses.

5. **Verify the Leads' Veracity**: Prior to assigning value to a lead, its veracity must be verified by validating the source of the generated data. Unreliable sources of data – such as hearsay, sensors with known high error rates, and systems

that have yet to be validated – degrade the lead and can possibly mislead the investigative team.

6. **Determine the Leads' Context**: In the discipline of network forensic investigations context means everything. An administrative server console with a known password may be immediately deemed to be a vulnerability, unless it is discovered the console is air-gapped, in a highly-secured area, and monitored by surveillance cameras 24-hours a day.

   The same rule applies to all activity within a network; investigators must understand normal activity (context) before abnormal activity can be identified and investigated.

Turning Leads into Indicators

Leads which have been verified as accurate have a unique set of characteristics that can signify malicious actions. These unique characteristics can be used as a foundation to create indicators of activity within a network. Validated leads can result in host-based indicators, network-based indicators, or a combination of both.

Network forensic investigators will be concerned with two specific types of indicators: *property-based* and *methodology-based*.

1. **Property-Based Indicators**: As the name implies, these types of indicators have a unique property that identifies them, such as a specific cryptographic hash or association with a particular registry key.

2. **Methodology-Based Indicators**: Indicators displaying certain behaviors or functionality outside the realm of normal network activity or configuration – such as unexpected executable files – are useful for scoping an incident and providing additional investigative leads.

Domain 11: *Initial Development of Leads*

The Life Cycle of Indicator Generation

Indicator generation is an iterative process with the goal of generating robust, sustainable signatures to generate reliable information. The process is relatively straightforward. Data taken from the initial lead is used to create indicators. The indicator is created and edited as needed based on verification of its validity, and then published to specific network sensors.

Indicator Verification: Challenges

It is important for network investigators to ensure that the properties of a new indicator do not identify the malware or activity solely at a specific point in the attack lifecycle. Fixation on one specific point may cause investigators to miss other critical data associated with a different point in the life cycle.

In the example listed below, consider the challenge of fixating on a signature of a known malware "dropper" and ignoring its role in the attack life cycle, and the ensuing damage that may occur.

1. Email is Sent with a Malicious Payload
2. The Payload is a Word Document with a "Dropper"
3. The User Opens the Word Document
4. (Includes a Second-Stage Malicious Executable)
5. The Primary Malware Removes the "Dropper"
6. The Second-Stage Malware Executes
7. The Signature of the "Dropper" is Rendered Ineffective

Indicator Verification: Considerations

It is important for network investigators to ensure the indicator analysis process identifies both the data relevant to the indicator, and how the data changes over time in the indicator itself. This level of understanding allows for the iterative creation and editing phases.

Listed below are considerations for the verification of effective signatures, and several potential sources that can be utilized in the verification process.

1. Examine the Payload Completely
2. Understand the Attack Life Cycle
3. Review the File Entry in the Prefetch Directory
4. Review the File Name in the MRU Registry Key
5. Review API Calls Logged in the Browser History
6. Review the DNS Cache Entry for the Hosting Site
7. Review the Second-Stage Malware File Metadata

Resolving Internal Leads

The key items for investigator case notes are actions taken and the dates on which those actions occurred; no automated process will help in this situation. Listed below are five general guidelines for network investigators conducting internal interviews and gathering leads in the incident environment.

1. Thoroughly Document all Statements
2. Allow the Interviewee to Tell a Story
3. Avoid Asking Leading Questions
4. Ask Open-Ended Questions (not "YES" or "NO")
5. Collect Facts Before Soliciting Opinions
6. Know When to Get Others Involved

Reporting Incidents to Law Enforcement Agencies (LEA's)

The primary justification for avoiding notification of an incident is simply to avoid a public relations issue. While notification of criminal acts involving network activity is rarely required – it is typically left to the discretion of the victimized organization as to whether or not official charges are pursued – there are many valid reasons to solicit the assistance of law enforcement agencies.

Domain 11: *Initial Development of Leads*

Listed below are several supporting law enforcement capabilities network investigators may wish to consider when confronted with serious incidents.

1. The Capacity to Investigate and Prosecute
2. LEA Subpoenas Generate Quicker Responses
3. Criminal Action at no Cost to the Victim Organization
4. LEA Search and Seizure Capabilities
5. LEA Criminal Cases Help Civilian Civil Cases
6. LEA Access to Aggregated Data from Many Sources
7. Foreign Malicious Action Requires Official Channels

LEA: Law Enforcement Agency

[This page intentionally left blank]

DOMAIN 11

Initial Development
of Leads

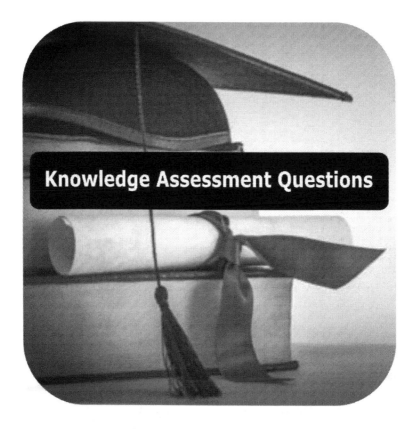

The following knowledge assessment questions are presented in true / false, multiple choice, and fill-in-the-blank formats. The correct answers are provided in an Answer Key at the end of this text. These questions may or may not be presented on the actual certification exam.

Domain 11: Knowledge Assessment Questions

An example of a _____-based indicator would be a cryptographic hash that could be cross-references against known hashes in a resource library.

A. Universal

B. Methodology

C. Performance

D. Property

E. None of the Above

Which of the following statements would **not** apply to a network investigator attempting to define leads of value?

A. Determine the Leads' Context

B. The Lead must have Sufficient Detail

C. The Lead must be Actionable

D. The Lead must be True

E. All of the Above

Forensic investigators should be aware that _____ when considering reporting a network incident to law enforcement.

A. Multiple Agencies Exist

B. Civil Cases Help Criminal Cases

C. Foreign Actions Require Informal Channels

D. Law Enforcement Presence Adds Validity to the Case

E. None of the Above

When a network investigator is conducting interviews and resolving internal leads, which of actions listed below is a best practice that should be followed?

A. Allow the Interviewee to Tell a Story

B. Document Important Statements

C. Collect Opinions Before Facts

D. Do not Involve Third-Parties

E. All of the Above

Domain 11: *Initial Development of Leads*

The final step taken by forensic investigators in the Life Cycle of Indicator Generation is to _____.
A. Publish Indicators
B. Edit Known Indicators
C. Gather Data from Initial Leads
D. Verify Known Indicators
E. None of the Above

What statement listed below does **not** represent a valid reason for a network investigator to seek out the assistance and involvement of law enforcement during an Incident Response?
A. Capacity to Investigate and Prosecute
B. Search and Seizure Capabilities
C. Civil Cases Help Criminal Cases
D. Subpoenas Generate Quicker Response
E. All of the Above

When resolving internal lead, forensic investigators should _____ to lessen the possibility of biased and misleading information.
A. Record Conversations
B. Require Written Statements
C. Remain Quiet
D. Avoid Leading Questions
E. None of the Above

What statement listed below is a valid reason for a network investigator to seek out the assistance and involvement of law enforcement during an Incident Response?
A. Capacity to Investigate and Prosecute
B. Search and Seizure Capabilities
C. Criminal Cases Help Civil Cases
D. Subpoenas Generate Quicker Response
E. All of the Above

Domain 11: *Initial Development of Leads*

An example of a _____-based indicator would be a portable executable file that creates an anomaly in a network information flow.

A. Universal

B. Methodology

C. Performance

D. Property

E. None of the Above

Which of the following statements would apply to a network investigator attempting to define leads of value?

A. Determine the Leads' Context

B. The Lead must be General

C. Only Come from Management

D. The Lead must be True

E. All of the Above

It is important for forensic investigators to ensure that the properties of a new indicator do not identify the malware or activity _____ at a specific point in the lifecycle.

A. Intermittently

B. Quickly

C. Randomly

D. Solely

E. All of the Above

Which of the choices listed below is a methodology-based indicator of interest to an investigator responding to a network incident?

A. Windows Registry Key

B. Unexpected Executable File

C. MD5 Cryptographic Hash

D. Unexplained Power Outage

E. All of the Above

Domain 11: *Initial Development of Leads*

Sorting the good leads from the bad is important, especially when the organization has a fully staffed team with ample time to conduct the investigation.

1. True

2. False

Indicator generation is an iterative process with a goal of generating robust, sustainable signatures to generate reliable information.

1. True

2. False

Leads can result in either host-based indicators or network-based indicators, but never a combination of both.

1. True

2. False

The key items for investigator case notes are personnel involved and the scope of the incident; automated processes will help streamline this situation.

1. True

2. False

Investigators must ensure the indicator verification process identifies data relevant to the indicator and how the data changes over time in the indicator itself.

1. True

2. False

The primary justification for avoiding notification is to avoid losing control of an investigation to law enforcement; additionally, notification of criminal acts is rarely required.

1. True

2. False

DOMAIN 12

Principles of
Live Data Collection

Domain 12: *Principles of Live Data Collection*

When to Perform a Live Response

Acquisition of data from live networks poses unique risks and challenges for network forensic investigators. At times those risks are acceptable and even necessary; at times, they are not.

The five questions listed below should serve as a guide and litmus test when determining if live response is an appropriate course of action.

Question #01:

Is there a reason to believe volatile data contains information critical to the investigation that is not present elsewhere?

Question #02:

Can the live response be executed in an ideal manner, minimizing any changes to the target system?

Question #03:

Is the number of affected systems large, making it infeasible to perform forensic duplication on all of them?

Question #04:

Is there a risk that forensic duplications will take an excessive amount of time, or potentially fail altogether?

Question #05:

Are there legal or other special considerations that make it a wise choice to preserve as much data as possible?

Live Response Challenges

There are serious potential challenges to performing a live response; the process may crash the system and/or destroy potential evidence. Unlike most digital forensic investigations in which single devices not connected to a network are examined, a mistake in a live network can have unforeseeable consequences. Prior to performing a live response, network forensic investigator should obtain answers to the five questions listed below and use them as criteria for their decisions.

1. **Has the Process been Tested on a Similar System?** If the process has not been tested on a system that is similar (and preferably identical) to the system in a live network environment, the investigator has no way of predicting how the system in question will respond to any process.

2. **Is the System Sensitive to Performance?** If the system in the network environment has bandwidth constraints, a fragile architecture, or is a legacy system requiring a specialized approach, network forensic investigators should know that in advance and adjust their collection methods accordingly.

3. **What is the Impact of a System Crash?** If a critical system in the network goes down unexpectedly because a process used by a network forensic investigator, the impact on the organization must be determined in advance. Disaster Recovery plans, accessible system back-ups, and other potential strategies should all be considered.

4. **Have all Stakeholders been Informed?** The potential impacts and challenges associated with live response demand stakeholders at various levels be informed of the process and its consequences. These stakeholders extend well beyond the C-Suit and include customers, suppliers, vendors, upstream logistical supply chains, downstream organizational dependencies, and a wide variety of other actors. These considerations are driven by legal issues as well as organizational issues.

5. **Has Formal and Written Approval been Received?** The owner of the risk, not the network forensic investigator, is ultimately responsible for any outcome impacting the organization. In a perfect world that would be apparent and immediate but, in many cases, blame and fault are

deflected and redirected by all involved parties. When lines of communication break down and those involved look for a scapegoat, the investigator with formal and written approval is typically immune from the "blame game."

Selecting a Live Response Tool

As techniques in live response and forensics evolve, available tools and procedures must be continually evaluated. Whether free or commercial, the tool selected must be the right tool for the job. In many cases more than one tool is required due to capability and contextual issues.

Regardless of the tools your investigative team chooses for live acquisition, the following six questions should establish a well-founded criteria for selection.

1. Is it Accepted in the Forensic Community?
2. Does it Address Common Operating Systems?
3. Does it Collect the Right Type of Data?
4. Is the Data Collection Time Acceptable?
5. Are the Procedures and Processes Configurable?
6. Is the Analysis Output Easily Understood?

Data Collection Considerations

Throughout an investigation, network forensic investigators must continuously evaluate what data to collect based on how quickly and effectively questions are answered. Based on the leads generated during any Incident Response, operational focus and mission priorities will always be subject to change.

Listed below are several data collection categories that must be evaluated on a regular basis by the Incident Response Team. Any changes to the categories below can change priority and focus quickly.

1. The Current Running System State

2. Network Connections and Processes
3. Contents of the System Memory
4. System Back-Ups (a Less Volatile Snapshot of the Past)
5. File Listings and System Logs
6. Application-Specific Data

Common Live Response Data

Although every operating system has unique sources of evidence, many areas of commonality exist between all of them. Some data is inherent to the specific operating system, and some data comes from common sources such as logging. It is important to note that operating system settings can greatly affect the available evidence, leaving some investigative questions unanswered.

The type of evidence collected by network forensic investigators will be dictated by the incident, environment, and goals of the Incident Response. While the list of live response data below is not meant to be all-inclusive, it does provide a general overview of data typically collected in this type of investigation.

1. Times, Dates, and Time Zones
2. The Operating System Version
3. General System Information
4. Boot-Up Services and Programs
5. Tasks Scheduled to Automatically Run
6. Local User Accounts and Group Members
7. NIC Details (IP, MAC Addresses)
8. Routing Information (ARP Tables and DNS Cache)
9. Network Connections and Processes
10. Currently Loaded Drivers and Modules
11. Files and Open Handles
12. Running Processes (PID and Runtime)
13. System Configuration Data
14. User Login History (Identifiers)
15. Standard System Log Data
16. List of all Installed Software

17. Relevant Application Log Data
18. Full File System Listing

Collection Best Practices

As with most tools, it is important to learn the correct way to use them. Live response tools are no exception. Planning and preparation are the key to successful deployment and the Incident Response Team would benefit from practicing their skills on a wide variety of multiple test systems.

Proper utilization of the tool to collect the required data, while having a minimal impact on the system, should be the goal of every investigator. Listed below are 11 common best practices every network forensic investigator should follow.

The application of these best practices will be dictated by the incident, environment, and goals of the Incident Response

Best Practice #01:

Document exactly what you do and when you do it. Note the difference between actual and system time. Do not forget to include time zones in notes.

Best Practice #02:

Treat the suspect system as "contaminated" – do not interact with it unless you have an established plan. Get on and off the system as quickly as possible.

Best Practice #03:

Use tools that minimize the impact on the target system. Avoid GUI-based collection tools; choose tools with a minimal memory profile and do not make excessive changes to the target system.

Best Practice #04:

Use tools that keep a log and use cryptographic checksums of their output as the output is created (not after the fact).

Best Practice #05:

Fully automate the collection process, perhaps eliminating the need for a human to interact with the suspect system.

Best Practice #06:

Make every effort to collect data in the order of volatility and take all measures to protect volatile data wherever possible.

Best Practice #07:

Treat all data you collect as evidence – be sure to follow data preservation procedures, including the creation of an evidence tag and chain of custody. Compute MD5 checksums of all collected evidence.

Best Practice #08:

Consider files on media you connect to the suspect system as lost to the attacker. Do not keep notes, indicators, documents, or reports on the media from which the live response will run.

Best Practice #09:

Consider any credentials you use as compromised. Use an account other than your primary, and change passwords frequently. Use two-factor authentication whenever possible.

Best Practice #10:

Do not take actions that will cause unnecessary modifications to the suspect system unless there is no other option. Doing so may destroy valuable evidence. Use external media and shares if and when possible.

Best Practice #11:

Do not use the suspect system to perform analysis; this can make the discernment of attacker activity from responder activity difficult. It can also make system changes and destroy potential evidence.

Domain 12: *Principles of Live Data Collection*

Example of a Live Response Tactic

The steps listed in this method minimizes changes to the suspect system and provides a convenient way for network forensic investigators to perform an incident response. Most forensic toolkits will deal with the issue of UAC (User Access Control), but the "Run as Administrator" may still be required to secure the required data.

Investigators must be prepared for any eventuality. Once again, the example listed below is only meant for consideration and to inspire network forensic investigators to create their own unique solutions to challenging events.

1. A Network Share Resides on a Dedicated Server
2. The Network Share Contains Two Files
3. The Server not Part of the Domain
4. Access Network Share with Throwaway Credentials
5. The First Share Folder is "Read-Only"
6. The First Folder also Contains the Forensic Toolkit
7. The Second Share Folder is Writable
8. The Second Folder Receives the Output
9. The Live Response is Run from the First Folder
10. Output is Directed to the Second Share Folder
11. Output is then Transferred to the Forensic Server
12. The Forensic Server is Secured with IAM Controls

[This page intentionally left blank]

DOMAIN 12

Principles of
Live Data Collection

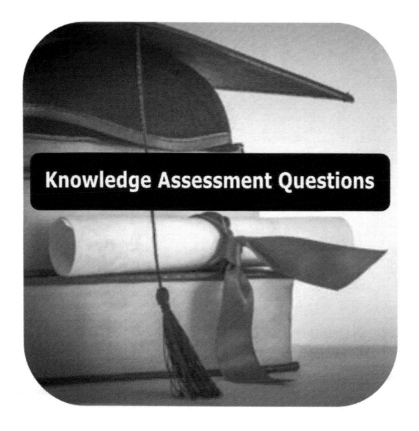

The following knowledge assessment questions are presented in true / false, multiple choice, and fill-in-the-blank formats. The correct answers are provided in an Answer Key at the end of this text. These questions may or may not be presented on the actual certification exam.

Domain 12: Knowledge Assessment Questions

One of the serious challenges faced by the forensic investigator when performing a live response is that the action could crash the system in question or _____.

A. Delete Evidence

B. Be Cost Prohibitive

C. Trigger Event Alerts

D. Force Unscheduled Upgrades

E. All of the Above

There are serious potential challenges to performing a live response. Which of the questions listed below would **not** apply to a network investigator considering a live response?

A. Has the Process Been Tested on a Similar System?

B. Has Verbal Approval Been Received?

C. What is the Impact of a System Crash?

D. Have all Stakeholders Been Informed?

E. All of the Above

Throughout an investigation, forensic investigators must continuously evaluate what data to collect based on how quickly and effectively _____.

A. Malware is Discovered

B. Systems are Rebuilt

C. Alerts are Reduced

D. Questions are Answered

E. All of the Above

Which of the questions listed below would **not** apply to a network investigator considering the selection of a live response tool?

A. Have the Results Been Successful in Court?

B. Is it Accepted by the Forensic Community?

C. Can it Collect the Right Type of Data?

D. Is the Analysis Output Easily Understood?

E. All of the Above

Domain 12: *Principles of Live Data Collection*

Some live response data is inherent to the specific operating system, and some live response data comes from common sources such as _____.
A. Network Documentation
B. Administrator Documentation
C. Vendor Support
D. Log Files
E. None of the Above

Which of the options listed below represents common live response data available to the network investigator?
A. Operating System Version Information
B. Boot-Up Services and Programs
C. Tasks Scheduled to Automatically Run
D. Local User Accounts and Group Members
E. All of the Above

Most forensic toolkits will successfully deal with UAC (User Access Control) but _____ may still be required to access a system.
A. Unique Passwords
B. "Run as Administrator"
C. Leadership Authorization
D. Two-Factor Authentication
E. None of the Above

Which of the following choices listed below is a challenge to an investigator attempting to perform a live response?
A. Automated Steps Replicated Manually
B. Cannot Connect Removable Media
C. Encrypted Network Streaming Tools
D. Network Share (SMB, CIFS, NFS)
E. All of the Above

Domain 12: *Principles of Live Data Collection*

Forensic network investigators are required to secure _____ before conducting any type of live response acquisition.

A. Verbal Approval

B. A Supervisor Signature

C. Written Approval

D. Specialized Software

E. None of the Above

Which of the statements listed below is **not** a best practice for an investigator engaged in the live response?

A. Minimize Impact on the System

B. Document Every Action Taken

C. Fully Automate the Collection Process

D. Treat the Suspect System as Compromised

E. None of the Above

As techniques in live response and forensics evolve, _____ and procedures must be continually evaluated.

A. Available Tools

B. Specialized Processes

C. Beta Technology

D. Unique Software

E. None of the Above

Which of the choices listed below can greatly affect the available evidence, leaving some questions unanswered?

A. User Login History (Identifiers)

B. Operating System Settings

C. Standard System Log Data

D. List of Installed Software

E. All of the Above

Domain 12: *Principles of Live Data Collection*

Compared to digital forensics, there is a significantly lower potential for challenges when conducting a live response during a network forensic investigation.

1. True

2. False

Throughout an investigation, investigators continuously evaluate what data to collect based on how quickly and effectively questions are answered.

1. True

2. False

It is important to note that operating system settings minimally affect the available evidence, allowing investigators to answer all questions required to produce leads.

1. True

2. False

Most forensic toolkits will deal with UAC (User Access Control), but the "Run as Administrator" may still be required.

1. True

2. False

As an industry best practice, make every effort to collect data in the order in which it is discovered and take all measures to protect non-volatile data wherever possible.

1. True

2. False

Do not use the suspect system to perform analysis; this can make the discernment of attacker activity from responder activity difficult.

1. True

2. False

DOMAIN 13

Investigating
Windows Systems

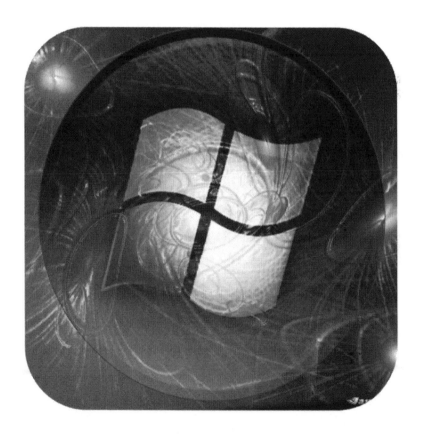

Windows System Overview

The Windows operating system is complex, multi-faceted, and can pose challenges to forensic investigators searching for evidence. The large number of directories and files found in many corporate environments – combined with the proprietary nature of the system that leaves many aspects undocumented – can create a flood of information and lead to mental overload when sorting through data.

The goal of this domain is to provide a general understanding of the primary sources of evidence on a typical Windows system and how it can be applied to solve common questions that typically arise. Listed below are the seven sources of forensic evidence which will be covered in this domain.

1. The NTFS (NT File System) Master File Table
2. Windows Prefetch
3. Event Logs
4. Scheduled Tasks
5. The Windows Registry
6. Memory Forensics
7. Persistence Mechanisms

Master File Table

Each NTFS volume will contain its own Master File Table stored within the volume root as a file named "$MFT." It is the primary source of metadata within NTFS and contains, either directly or indirectly, everything about a file stored on that volume. Just a few examples of valuable metadata include timestamps, the size of the file in bytes, file attributes (such as permissions), the parent directory, and file contents.

Each partition and/or drive on the system will have its own Master File Table. The existing metadata is not accessible directly using the Windows interface; it requires raw disk access using forensic software. When the Master File Table is acquired the investigator has the "keys to the data kingdom" – including deleted files.

Master File Table Evidence

NTFS defines how space is allocated and utilized, how files are created and deleted, and how metadata is stored and updated. The first 16 entries in the MFT contain a core set of artifacts that may potentially provide information crucial to an investigation. These core artifacts are listed below.

1. Type of Record (File or Directory)
2. Record Number (Identifies the MFT Entry)
3. Parent Record Number
4. Active and Inactive Flags (Deleted Files and Directories)
5. Attributes (File Metadata: Timestamps, Location, Size)

Identifying Deleted Files

Every entry in the Master File Table contains a *flag* which indicates whether the entry is *active* or *inactive*. When a file is deleted the MFT sets the flag to inactive, indicating that space is available to store new files. Although the flag has been set to inactive it still points location on the disk.

The data itself still remains in that space until it is overwritten by new data. Until that time the data is recoverable. The length of time deleted data remains on a disk before being overwritten depends on the operating system volume and the environment in which it operates.

Analyzing Timestamps

File timestamps are among the most important metadata stored in the Master File Table for forensic investigators. They are the foundation upon which investigative timelines are established. These timestamps are typically referred to as "MACE" times.

1. **M**odified: Time the File was Last Changed
2. **A**ccessed: Time the File was Last Read
3. **C**reated: Time the File was First Created
4. **E**ntry Modified: Time the MFT Entry was Changed

228

Each entry in the Master File Table will have two attributes containing MACE timestamps: the *Standard Information* attribute ($S1) and the *FileName* attribute ($FN). The $S1 contains various codes, identifiers and pointers; the $FN contains the name of the file, the file size, and the parent directory record number.

Overview: "Time-Stomping"

Malicious actors know the value of investigative timelines and make attempts to intentionally change timestamps to disrupt investigative efforts. It is common for malware "droppers" to automate this process when compromising systems. Applications have access to $S1 timestamps making it easy for users to change their values. There is no direct access to the $FN timestamps – raw disk access is required – making it much more difficult to manipulate this value.

Malicious actors employ a strategy called *time-stomping* to overcome the challenge of changing both the $S1 and $FN to matching values of their choosing. An overview of this process is listed below.

1. Set the $S1 timestamp to a chosen value
2. Move the file to a new directory within the same volume
3. Set the $S1 timestamp to a chosen value again
4. Move the file to its original location
5. Set the $S1 timestamp value again

When a file is moved to a different location within the same volume the Windows operating systems uses the existing $S1 timestamp to set the $FN timestamp for the new Master File Table entry. Changing the file location allows a manipulated $S1 timestamp to create a manipulated $FN timestamp. Returning the file to the original location and changing the $S1 timestamp again to match the manipulated $FN timestamp ensures both values match.

Unfortunately for the malicious actors – and fortunately for forensic investigators – other sources of timeline evidence such as event logs, the Windows Registry, and prefetch analysis can be used to reveal the true $FN timestamp and defeat this tactic.

Resident Data

The $DATA attribute within the Master File Table typically provides a listing of the clusters on a disk wherein a files' contents reside. However, smaller files (under 700 bytes) are stored in the attribute itself. When this occurs a *resident* flag is set in the Master File Table to indicate this location.

If a file is small enough to be resident but then exceeds resident limits over time it will be flagged as *non-resident*, relocated to a different location on the disk, and be flagged with a new pointer to the file clusters. After the files have been moved, portions of the original file may still be contained in the $DATA attribute than can be beneficial to the investigation.

INDX Attributes

While a Master File Table entry only tracks the parent record number of a file, the INDX attribute tracks all the cluster that make up the file in a directory. When files are deleted or reduced in size, the allocation attribute is not reduced automatically. This results in slack space when the file trees are reorganized which may contain portions of the original file.

A benefit of the INDX attribute entries – including entries existing in slack space – is that they contain the same metadata as a FileName attribute in the Master File Table. Examples of this metadata are listed below.

1. File Name
2. Parent Directory MFT Number
3. All Four MACE Timestamps
4. The Physical and Logical File Size

Change Logs

NTFS is a recoverable and journaled file system, so it maintains several logs to track changes made to directories and files. The data in these logs is used to reverse system operations when crashes occur and record evidence of file system activity as well. This is useful to forensic investigators when malicious actors delete files to obscure their actions.

The two logs of primary investigative importance are the *$Logfile* and the *$UsnJrnl*. The $Logfile tracks any activity that makes changes to the structure of a volume such as CRUD operations (Create, Read, Update, and Delete) and the altering of metadata. The $UsnJrnl, when it exists on a volume, provides a high-level change summary including events, file identifiers, and timestamps of the corresponding changes.

Volume Shadow Copies (VSC)

Volume Shadow Copies provide a mechanism for maintaining point-in-time copies of files on an entire volume (aka, "snapshots" and "restore points"). They can be created on local and external (removable or network) volumes by any Windows component that uses this technology, such as when creating a scheduled Windows Backup or automatic System Restore point.

Their benefit to forensic investigators is that they allow the recovery of files and Windows registry keys which provides an advantage when searching for modified or deleted files. The VSC happens automatically as a background process on running systems as well as being initiated manually by users of the system. Once a known timeline has been established the VSC in closest proximity to the event of interest may yield crucial information.

Prefetch

Prefetch is a performance optimization feature that Microsoft created for its operating system to reduce boot and application loading times. The Windows Cache Manager – a component of the memory management systems – monitors the data and code of all running processes.

It specifically focuses on the first two minutes of boot processes and the first ten seconds of application launch processes. The Cache Manager and the Task Scheduler coordinate with each other to write trace results to the Prefetch function. The stored traces speed up the process the next time the user boots the system or launches one of the monitored applications.

The traces written to Prefetch may provide investigators with useful information regarding applications and processes initiated by a user. The value of this data applies more to host machines than those operating larger networks. The Prefetch function is limited to 128 entries that are cyclically overwritten; in larger networks the Prefetch traces may only exist for a few seconds.

Prefetch Analysis

Prefetch files serve as a record of programs that have executed on a system, regardless of whether the original executable is still on the disk. If the trace data has not been overwritten investigators will have access to the information listed below.

1. Proof that an Application Ran
2. The Time that an Application Ran
3. The Number of Times that an Application Ran
4. The Path from which an Application Ran
5. The Exact Residence on the Disk
6. All Application Dependencies Required for Execution
7. All Files Use for Input and Output

Event Logs

Event logs are generated by the system-wide monitoring and auditing capabilities built into the Microsoft operating system. The logs are designed to monitor and record the types of events listed below.

1. Successful and/or Failed Logon Attempts
2. The Origin of the Logon Attempts
3. All System Services (Start and Stop)
4. Specific Application Usage
5. Alterations to the Audit Policy

    6. Any Changes to User Permissions

    7. All Installed Application Events

Event Log Evidence

All versions of Windows operating systems maintain three categories of "core" event logs: "Application," "System," and "Security." The *Application Log* monitors errors and reporting, the *System Log* monitors services and changes, and the *Security Log* monitors authentication and security. These log files are stored in a proprietary format (.EVT) and can only be read and examined with special tools.

Understanding Logon Events

Most Windows operating system forensic investigations will include the monitoring and analyzing of logon events (successful and unsuccessful). These events are monitored by the Security Log, within which investigators will find 14 fields of particular interest. A high-level perspective of the benefits of analyzing logon events is provided below.

    1. Prove Legitimate User Access

    2. Prove Malicious Remote Access

    3. Monitor Failed Logon Attempts

    4. Identify Brute Force Events

    5. Determine How a Compromised System was Utilized

Process Tracking

Process tracking, also known as process auditing, generates an event in the Security Event Log every time a process is executed or terminated. If this functionality is being utilized on the system in question – it is not enabled by default – investigators will have access to the information listed below.

    1. Full Path to the Executable on the Disk

2. Process ID
3. Parent Process ID
4. Associated Logon ID
5. Actions Executed by the User
6. Actions Executed within a Period of Time

Scheduled Tasks

The *Windows Task Scheduler* provides the ability to automatically execute programs at a specific date and time (or recurring dates and times). System applications can create tasks using the Windows API (Application Programming Interface) for a variety of reasons such as checking for software patches and updates.

Users can also create scheduled tasks manually using the Task Scheduler which is why this functionality is attractive to malicious actors. No "helper utilities" are required to program tasks which lessens the likelihood of detection. An examination of the Windows Task Manager will provide the information listed below.

1. Running Processes
2. System Performance (CPU Usage)
3. Application History
4. Start-Up Programs
5. System Users
6. System Details
7. System Services

Windows Registry Evidence

The *Windows Registry* serves as the primary database of configuration data for the Windows operating system and applications that are running on it. It is comprised of a number system and user-specific "hives" which are stored on a single file on the disk.

The information within these files is not human readable; special software is required to access and interpret the data. The data contained within these hives may prove to be valuable during an investigation as it provides significant insight into the users' activity on the system. In addition to system hives, there are several *root registry keys* that can contain valuable information as well. The primary keys of interest are listed below.

1. HKEY_LOCAL_MACHINE (HKLM)
2. HKEY_USERS (HKU)
3. HKEY_CURRENT_USER (HKCU)
4. HKEY_CURRENT_CONFIG (HKCC)
5. HKEY_CLASSES_ROOT

Investigators will need to use a forensic imaging or acquisition tool with raw disk access to copy registry hives while the system is booted.

Registry Analysis

The evidence that can be recovered from the Windows Registry during most forensic investigations can be both invaluable and voluminous. The four primary areas of interest to investigators are listed below.

1. System Configuration Registry Keys
2. Shim Cache
3. Auto-Run Registry Keys
4. Windows Services

System Configuration Registry Keys

By examining the correct keys, investigators can recover everything from the operating system installation date to current firewall policies and user groups. Some of these keys are encoded, not easily human readable, and require specialized tools to read and analyze. Examples of the types of information which can be acquired from the System Configuration Registry keys are listed below.

Domain 13: *Investigating Windows Systems*

1. Network, User, and Security Settings
2. Basic System Information
3. Network Information
4. User and Security Information

Shim Cache

Shim cache allows Windows to track executable files and scripts that may require special compatibility settings to properly run. The cache is maintained within the systems' kernel memory and is serialized to the Windows Registry when the system is powered down. The types of information available to investigators is based upon the version of the Microsoft version being used but typically include the data listed below.

1. The File Name with a Full Paths
2. Last Modified Date of the $S1 Timestamp
3. Size of the File in Bytes
4. If a File Ran on the System

Another benefit the shim cache offers investigators is that it retains more entries than prefetch functionality before overwriting the data. Prefetch retains 128 entries while the him cache maintains 1,024 entries.

Auto-Run Keys

Auto-run keys – also known as auto-start extensibility points – ensure that Windows executable files, DLL's, and other components load correctly upon the system boot and user login. They are just one of thousands of registry-based persistence mechanisms found in a Windows operating system.

Malicious actors will modify existing keys (or add their own auto-run keys to the Registry) once a system has been compromised to ensure malware is automatically loaded when the system is booted up.

Memory Forensics

Windows maintains several important (and highly volatile) artifacts that can only be recovered while a system is powered "ON." While it is possible to access a portion of this data using a Windows API, the use of forensic tools to access and reconstructing the contents of memory yields the most reliable, tamper-resistant results during forensic investigations.

The Windows memory system is configured allocate memory to RAM (volatile) and a portion to the disk (non-volatile) to the disk if needed under certain conditions. Several examples of the types of useful data that can be obtained are listed below.

1. Running Processes and Resources
2. Active Network Connections
3. Loaded Drivers
4. User Credentials (Obfuscated and Clear)
5. Previous Console Commands

Process Memory Analysis

A *process listing* reveals "what is running" on a Windows system, using tools such as Windows *Task Manager* and the SysInternals *Process Explorer*. Using forensic tools, Executive Process Blocks (a kernel data structure) can be used to access, collect, and analyze the investigative information listed below.

1. Process ID (PID)
2. Parent ID
3. Process Name
4. Process Path
5. Process Start and Stop Times
6. Number of Threads and Handles

Additional Memory Artifacts

The number and type of artifacts that can be recovered from memory continuously expands as technology, tools, and systems evolve. However, regardless of the size and complexity of the systems investigators will encounter in the future, the forensic memory artifacts listed below will continue to remain valuable.

Persistence Mechanisms

Persistence mechanisms refers to a broad range and category of registry keys, file paths, and other components that load and run executable code. An auto-run programmed to execute during a system boot or a user logon would be a common example of a persistence mechanism.

Although many of the mechanisms are based in the Windows Registry they can exist independently in other areas of the system. Malicious actors who have successfully compromised a system may utilize legitimate processes to place persistence mechanisms – such as backdoors and malicious code – in locations such as the Recycle Bin, temporary file folders, or other unobtrusive directories that go largely unnoticed by most users.

DOMAIN 13

Investigating
Windows Systems

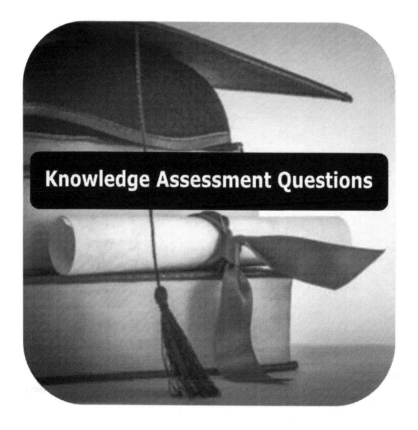

The following knowledge assessment questions are presented in true / false, multiple choice, and fill-in-the-blank formats. The correct answers are provided in an Answer Key at the end of this text. These questions may or may not be presented on the actual certification exam.

Domain 13: Knowledge Assessment Questions

Each NTFS volume will contain its own _____ stored within the volume root as a file named "$MFT."

A. Permissions Directory

B. Master Record Listing

C. Primary Service Directory

D. Master File Table

E. None of the Above

Which choice listed below describes a function or characteristic of Volume Shadow Copies (VSC)?

A. Automated Processes Trigger Snapshots

B. Times are Changed Between Intervals

C. Availability of Data is Unlimited

D. Cannot be Used for File Recovery

E. None of the Above

The benefit of _____ entries (including slack) is they contain the same metadata as a FileName attribute in the Master File Table.

A. INDX Attribute

B. Resident Data

C. Change Log

D. Event Log

E. None of the Above

Which choice listed below describes a function or characteristic of the Resident Data attribute?

A. Always Sequential (Contiguous)

B. Contains File Data when Assembled

C. Contiguous Clusters are "Fragmented"

D. Files >800 Bytes in Data Attribute

E. None of the Above

_____ provide a mechanism for maintaining point-in-time copies of files on an entire volume (aka, "snapshots" and "restore points").

A. Event ID's

B. Shim Cache Processes

C. Prefetch Processes

D. Volume Shadow Copies

E. None of the Above

Which choice listed below describes a function or characteristic of the Prefetch performance optimization mechanism?

A. Resides in the Windows Task Manager

B. Runs in the First 5 Minutes of the Boot Process

C. Increases Boot and Application Load Times

D. Limited to 128 Entries

E. None of the Above

All versions of Windows systems maintain three categories of "core" event logs: "_____," "System," and "Security."

A. User

B. Remote

C. Logon

D. Application

E. None of the Above

Which choice listed below describes a characteristic of an event logged in the Windows Security Event log generated by the process tracking function?

A. Settings are Enabled by Default

B. Full Path to the Executable on the Disk

C. Actions are Retained for an Indefinite Time

D. Logs Actions Executed by the O/S

E. None of the Above

Domain 13: *Investigating Windows Systems*

The Windows _____ provides the ability to automatically execute programs at a specific date and time (or recurring).

A. Process Explorer

B. Task Scheduler

C. Shim Cache

D. Registry Keys

E. None of the Above

Which choice listed below describes a function or characteristic of System Configuration Registry Keys?

A. All Keys are Encoded

B. Easily Human Readable

C. LIVE: Access Restricted to "USER"

D. Network, User, and Security Settings

E. None of the Above

_____ refers to a broad range and category of registry keys, file paths, and other components that load and run executable code.

A. Persistence Mechanisms

B. Alternate Data Streams

C. Parent Directory Files

D. Volume Shadow Copies

E. None of the Above

Which choice listed below describes a characteristic of potential evidence that can be found in the Windows Registry?

A. Significant Insight into User Activity

B. Hive is Stored in Multiple Files on the Disk

C. Files are Human Readable

D. Nine Main Windows Registry Hives

E. None of the Above

NTFS (NT File System) defines how space is allocated and utilized, how files are created and deleted, and how metadata is stored and updated.

1. True

2. False

File timestamps (MACE) are among the most important metadata stored in the temporary Recycle Bin for forensic investigators.

1. True

2. False

The benefit of INDX attribute entries (including slack) is they contain the same metadata as a FileName attribute in the Master File Table.

1. True

2. False

Volume shadow copies are a performance optimization mechanism Microsoft introduced to reduce boot and application loading times.

1. True

2. False

The Registry serves as the primary database of configuration data for the Windows operating system and applications that run on it.

1. True

2. False

By examining the correct Security Control Reinforcement Keys, you can recover everything from the system O/S installation date to current firewall policies and user groups.

1. True

2. False

DOMAIN 14

Investigating Applications

Domain 14: *Investigating Applications*

Overview: Investigating Applications

When examining network forensic evidence, it is common to find artifacts that are not part of – or dependent upon – the operating system. Applications are critical sources of evidence that provide a large amount of data in a wide variety of formats. Listed below are sources of evidence which will prove useful to investigators.

1. User Applications (Browsers)
2. Service Applications (Servers)
3. Web Applications, Email, and IM Clients

Windows: Application Data Storage

Although applications can store data in custom locations, most operating systems have a standard naming and storage convention. Windows operating systems tend to share common default locations which have the potential to yield many useful artifacts. A few examples of these default locations and the evidence contained in them are listed below.

1. Application Installation Directory
2. Application Data Directories
3. Uninstall Information in the Registry
4. Registry Configuration Data Locations

General Investigative Methods

The purpose of investigating an application is to determine what forensic artifacts it creates and how the artifacts may be beneficial to the investigation. Most of the popular forensic tools have the ability to assist in performing this function.

Another means by which applications can be investigated is by conducting researching using respected sources such as *Forensic Focus* and the *Forensic Wiki*. Investigators can also perform their own testing and directed research on an application, a skill that aligns and overlaps with the skills required to perform malware triage successfully.

Domain 14: *Investigating Applications*

High-Level Investigative Process

As mentioned previously, investigators can perform their own directed testing and research on an application to determine what useful artifacts it may generate. Before expending effort, check if your preferred forensic suite supports processing the application data that is relevant to the investigation. If not, the steps listed below are considered to be a best practice for initiating a high-level investigative process.

1. Configure an Appropriate Environment
2. Obtain the Application to be Investigated
3. Configure the Required Instrumentation
4. Perform the Installation of the Application
5. Execute the Application
6. Review the Instrumentation Data
7. Adjust the Instrumentation and Re-Test the Application as needed

Investigating Web Browsers

Web browsers are applications that retrieve, process, and present data, and are currently the most popular computer applications in mainstream use. Browsers generate may system artifacts which have the potential to provide crucial evidence to investigators. The three primary sources of web browser evidence are listed below.

1. History: URL's, Dates, and Times
2. Cache: Stored Local Copies of Data
3. Cookies: Preferences and Sessions

Internet Explorer

Internet Explorer (IE) is a web browser maintained by Microsoft, mostly supported in larger enterprises, and installed by default on the MS operating system. Listed below are the seven primary types of data within the IE browser that may contain potentially valuable artifacts that can be used as evidence.

Domain 14: *Investigating Applications*

1. Autocomplete (Typed Searches)
2. Typed URL's
3. Preferences
4. Cache
5. Cookies
6. Bookmarks
7. History

Google Chrome

Google Chrome was launched in 2008 and has steadily grown in popularity to become number one of the top three most widely used web browsers. Listed below are the seven primary types of data within the Chrome browser that may contain potentially valuable artifacts and evidence.

1. History   (Typed, Visited, and Transitions)
2. Cache   (Use to Reconstruct Visited Websites)
3. Cookies   (Location, Usernames, and Email Addresses)
4. Downloads   (URL, Size, Time, and Opened)
5. Autofill   (Enabled by Default / aka "Form Data")
6. Bookmarks   (JSON Files Stored in a Plain Text Format)
7. Preferences (Extensions, Plugins, and Synced Accounts)

Mozilla Firefox

Firefox was released in 2004 and challenged Internet Explorer's (version 6) dominance with 60 million downloads within nine months. According to sources tracking web browser market share it is currently ranked the third most popular browser based on usage. The types of artifacts available to investigators is similar to those listed above for Google's *Chrome* browser.

Settings in Firefox allow the user to clear all browser history on demand and automatically. Although other browsers have the same capability, Firefox actively promotes and encourages the use of this functionality as a privacy feature for its users.

Investigating E-Mail Clients

There are many types of security incidents and investigations in which e-mail is a key source of evidence for network forensic investigators. It is a popular tool for malicious actors to use in "phishing" campaigns, social engineering, "scareware" campaigns, and financial scams. In many cases email addresses are a direct target; stolen accounts are valuable when used for illicit communication and transferring unauthorized data.

All e-mail is comprised of two primary components: the *body* (text and attachments) and the *header* (sender and receiver information, date, subject, and transporting server data). The body of the e-mail is typically encoded in MIME (Multipurpose Internet Mail Extensions) and the proprietary headers tend to be complex to decode.

Web-Based E-Mail

Surveys indicate that web-based e-mail (such as *Gmail*, *Outlook*, *Hotmail*, and *Yahoo!*) now accounts for more than 50% of all e-mail clients in use, and 75% of users check their e-mail on mobile devices (*Apple iPhones* and *Android* devices). This presents many significant challenges for investigators as data is not store on the local system and very few artifacts exist outside of the users' browser. Even with specialized forensic tools such as *Cellebrite* and *Oxygen*, physical and logical acquisition efforts can be daunting.

Microsoft Outlook for Windows

Although e-mail versions for both Windows and Apple operating systems exist, the most common encountered by investigators tends to be Windows. Microsoft *Outlook* supports POP, IMAP, MX, and HTTP-based protocols and offers many extensions to increase the clients' capabilities.

As is the custom of Microsoft, the data storage functionality is proprietary. Investigators must determine the default profile to access information as the client allows users to configure multiple profiles. Deleting a user profile does not delete the profiles' data.

Domain 14: *Investigating Applications*

Investigating Instant Message Clients

Instant Message (IM) clients provide a way for individuals to have the ability to communicate with each other in (near) real time. They can be used for two-way communication, multiple user communication, and group chat sessions. The capabilities listed below – and the potential artifacts they generate – are of interest to investigators.

1. File Transfers
2. Voice Chat
3. Video Conferencing
4. Voice-to-Telephone Chat
5. Saved Voicemail

Instant Message Investigative Methodology

Frequent updates of IM technology requires thoroughly testing each client to ensure the results returned from any tool or method are accurate. Listed below are several guidelines and factors investigators should consider when investigating these clients.

1. Create a Documented Testing Methodology
2. Create an Appropriate Test Environment (O/S and version)
3. Understand Common IM Technologies
4. HTML: Logs are Saved as HTML Files
5. XML: Used by Windows Messenger Logs
6. SQLite: Used for Mozilla-Based Applications
7. SOAP*: Used for Yahoo! and Gmail Artifacts

* *Simple Object Access Protocol* (SOAP) is used by e-mail clients to access mailboxes.

Facebook Chat

The popular social media site Facebook provides a built-in web-based text and video chat client called *Facebook Messenger* which allows users to communicate others on their "Friends List."

251

Domain 14: *Investigating Applications*

The functionality provided by this service takes place on a web-based client which does not require a local installation of software.

All user data is logged by default. However, these logs are stored on Facebook servers, not locally on the users' system. This makes it challenging for investigators unless they have user access to the client.

Facebook Chat: Log Format

Facebook chat messages contained in logs are formatted in *JavaScript Object Notation* (JSON), a human-readable text format. If a forensic investigator is able to access the *Messenger* user account, a tool that can parse Facebook chat messages, along with many other evidence items, is *Internet Evidence Finder* (IEF).

The log data is stored under the "MSG" tag and contains several fields that may prove valuable to the forensic investigation. Listed below are the primary fields of interest.

1. "text"   (Includes the Body of the Message)
2. "messageID"   (A Facebook Identifier)
3. "time"   (Time of the Message in UTC)
4. "from"   (Facebook ID of the Sender)
5. "to"   (Facebook ID of the Recipient)
6. "from name"   (Plain Text Format)
7. "to name"   (Plain Text Format)
8. "sender offline" (*False* if the Person is Online)

DOMAIN 14

Investigating Applications

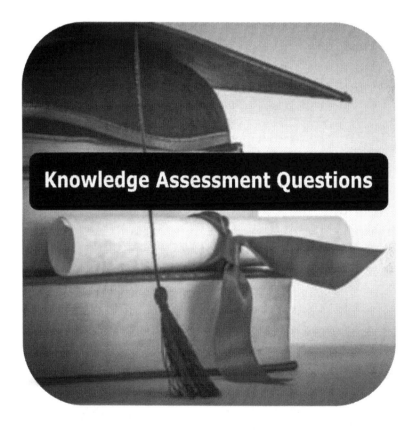

The following knowledge assessment questions are presented in true / false, multiple choice, and fill-in-the-blank formats. The correct answers are provided in an Answer Key at the end of this text. These questions may or may not be presented on the actual certification exam.

Domain 14: Knowledge Assessment Questions

While examining forensic evidence, it is common to find artifacts that are not part of – or dependent upon – the _____.

A. System Memory

B. File System

C. Directory System

D. Operating System

E. None of the Above

What choice listed below describes a function or characteristic likely to be encountered by forensic investigators when investigating web browsers?

A. History: Preferences and Sessions

B. Cache: URL's, Data, and Time

C. Cookies: Stored Local Copies

D. Creates Many System Artifacts

E. None of the Above

If an application is not _____, perform research to determine what artifacts may be useful and where they may be located.

A. Properly Licensed

B. Well-Documented

C. Launching Properly

D. Remaining Stable

E. None of the Above

What choice listed below describes an area of interest to forensic investigators when investigating the Google Chrome web browser?

A. Cache (Database, Not Text Files)

B. Cookies (Typed, Visited, and Transitions)

C. Autofill (Enabled by Default)

D. History (User Data\Default\Cache)

E. None of the Above

Domain 14: *Investigating Applications*

_____ are applications that retrieve, process, and present data, and are currently the most popular computer applications in mainstream use.

A. Search Engines

B. Word Processors

C. Office Suites

D. Web Browsers

E. None of the Above

What choice listed below describes a function or characteristic associated with Mozilla's web browser Firefox?

A. Different File Names Across the O/S's

B. Configurable Settings to Clear History

C. Stored in Directories in the Admin Profile

D. New Version Every 8-10 Weeks

E. None of the Above

_____ is a web browser maintained by Microsoft, mostly supported in larger enterprises, and installed by default on the MS O/S.

A. Mozilla Firefox

B. Google Chrome

C. Internet Explorer

D. Microsoft Edge

E. None of the Above

What choice listed below describes a function or characteristic associated with Microsoft Outlook for Windows?

A. POP, IMAP, MX, and HTTP-Based

B. Uses Open-Source Data Storage

C. Add-Ins Limit the Client Capabilities

D. Deleting a Profile Deletes User Data

E. None of the Above

_____ was launched in 2008, and steadily grown in popularity to become number one of the top three most widely used web browsers.

A. Internet Explorer

B. Google Chrome

C. Microsoft Edge

D. Mozilla Firefox

E. None of the Above

What choice listed below describes a function or characteristic associated with the Facebook Chat application?

A. Local Installation of the Software

B. Logs are Stored on the User System

C. Challenging Without Account Access

D. Does not Log Data by Default

E. None of the Above

_____ clients provide a way for individuals to have the ability to communicate with each other in (near) real time.

A. Email

B. Voicemail

C. Instant Message

D. Browser

E. None of the Above

What choice listed below describes a function or characteristic associated with the Facebook's Messenger application?

A. Requires Local Installation of the Software

B. Allows Communication with "Friends List"

C. Takes Place Through a Server-Based Client

D. Logs are Stored on the User System

E. None of the Above

Domain 14: *Investigating Applications*

While examining forensic evidence, it is uncommon to find artifacts that are not part of – or dependent upon – the operating system.
1. True
2. False

Before expending effort, check if your preferred forensic suite supports processing the application data that is relevant to the investigation.
1. True
2. False

Apple's Safari was launched in 2008, and steadily grown in popularity to become number one of the top three most widely used web browsers.
1. True
2. False

Surveys indicate that web and mobile-based e-mail now account for more than 50% of all e-mail clients.
1. True
2. False

Facebook Chat messages in memory are formatted in Extensible Markup Language (XML), a text format that is not human readable.
1. True
2. False

A tool that can parse Facebook Chat messages, along with many other evidence items, is Internet Evidence Finder (IEF).
1. True
2. False

DOMAIN 15

Static and Dynamic Malware Triage

Domain 15: *Static and Dynamic Malware Triage*

Introduction to Malware Triage

Most people call any program that an attacker uses to their advantage, including publicly available tools, "malware." Calling all programs an attacker uses "malware" is really not a good idea because the term is too generic.

Investigators are better served by further categorizing malware in their description – such as *backdoor*, *privilege escalator*, and *port redirector* – because it better describes the attackers' goals and the function of the malware itself.

Additionally, a detailed description is more likely to protect others conducting triage from inherent dangers associated with the task. Listed below are points all investigators should consider when preparing to handle any type of malware.

1. Dangers Exist when Performing Triage
2. Analysis on Unknown Files is Risky
3. Analysis of Known Malware is Risky
4. One Might Unknowingly Infect Their Own System
5. Malware Might Cause Extensive Damage

Malware Handling Procedures: General

Never triage malware on a primary operating system; make every effort to conduct all triage in a virtual environment. The intelligence generated by the investigator should be actionable; if not, the process will simply waste time.

If the results are actionable, they can help generate indicators of compromise that can then be used to sweep a larger population of systems. Listed below are a number of best practices which may decrease the likelihood of unintentional infection.

1. Use a Virtual Environment for Triage
2. Ensure the Virtual Environment is Isolated
3. Create and Load a Known Clean Snapshot
4. Use a Modern Version of the Primary O/S

5. Ensure the System is Fully Patched and Updated
6. Keep the Virtualization Software Updated
7. Disable all "Convenience" Features
8. Disable the "Preview View" Functionality
9. Disable Autorun and Automount Features
10. Revert the VM to a Known Clean Image After the Triage

Malware Handling Procedures: Specific

Protocols should address all aspects of dealing with malware, from the pre-analysis stage to final storage or disposition when case is closed. Listed below are several safety considerations that should be incorporated into malware triage protocols.

1. Prominently Label the Transport Media
2. Use a CD/DVD with Large and Bold Fonts
3. Handle as a "Non-Privileged" User
4. Underscore Malware File Extensions
5. Store in a Directory that Denies Execution
6. Store in a Password Protected and/or Encrypted Archive
7. Only Allow "Non-Privileged" Access
8. Use a Common Password: "INFECTED" (Awareness)

Malware Handling Documentation

Investigators should pass on details that will help the triage process, and analysts should question investigators when details are lacking. Some questions may seem unrelated or too simplistic to be useful, but they provide contextual facts that cannot be determined by analysis alone.

Listed below are several questions that should be considered and communicated when handling any malware documentation.

1. How was the File Identified?
2. What is the Operating System Version?
3. What is the Original File Name and Directory?

4. Is the File "Known"? (Checksum Match)
5. Are Other Related Files Present?
6. Do Artifacts Exist that Identify the Malware?
7. Does Evidence Exist of Command-Line Execution?
8. Does Evidence Exist of "C2" Mechanisms?
9. Is the Malware Believed to be Persistent?
10. Were the Items MACED at the Time of Installation?
11. Were Additional Types of Malware Found?
12. Do Attributes of a Particular Threat Exist?
13. Is the Attacker Active and the Incident Ongoing?

Malware Distribution

When investigative teams are in the middle of a crisis and looking for answers, it is difficult to resist the help third-party providers may offer. While they can provide value, distributing malware to them comes with potentially serious risks. The malware may contain information identifying the victim (through customized scripts) and sensitive information (such as usernames, passwords, and internal proxy server authentication data).

While the third-party may be well-known and respected, the victim does not know who is handling their data. Many triage sites are run by antivirus vendors and may take actions which inadvertently tip off attackers and disrupt investigation and remediation efforts. Once the attacker knows the teams' investigative tactics, they are more likely to change theirs if they believe their malware has been discovered.

If and when malware is provided to third-parties, ensure it is done on terms favorable to the investigation. Listed below are several questions to consider when preparing to submit malware to third-parties, knowing this could potentially alert attackers to the investigative teams activities.

1. Is a Disaster Recovery Plan in Place?
2. Is the Disaster Recovery Plan Tested and Effective?
3. Is the Victim Aware Destructive Actions may be Taken?

4. Is the Impact of the Destructive Actions Known?
5. Can the Organization Recover from the Actions?

Accessing Malicious Web Sites

In general, investigators should not access malicious sites for many reasons, some of which can affect the victim organization as well as others. Additionally, a well-intentioned investigator may be breaking the law if retaliatory actions are taken, as stated by the *Computer Fraud & Abuse Act* (Title 18, Section 1030).

Listed below are several unintentional consequences to consider prior to visiting any known malicious website.

1. The Investigators' System may Become Infected
2. The Investigators' Actions may Alert Attackers
3. The "Malicious Site" may be a Victim Themselves
4. The Investigators may be Identified as Targets

The Physical Triage Environment

It is an industry best practice to perform malware triage in appropriate and formally designated triage environments. When performing triage in a physical environment – one in which the operating system resides directly on hardware – ensure the device is segregated from the network ("Air-Gapped").

Physical access to the environment should be restricted, and the system should be returned to a clean known state once the malware triage has been concluded.

The Virtual Triage Environment

A virtual machine requires virtualization software and a physical system to host the triage environment, although the triage process itself does not require physical hardware. Performance of the virtual environment can be increased by ensuring the memory and hard drive capacity are upgraded.

One disadvantage of a virtual environment is the malware being analyzed may be "virtual aware" and not function as it would on a physical system, making analysis difficult. However, there are several benefits listed below that make virtual environments ideal for malware triage.

1. A Virtual Machine Configuration is Highly Flexible
2. Virtual Machines Eliminate Resource Contention
3. Virtual Machines are Easy to Return to a Known State
4. Virtual Machines Eliminate Cross-Contamination

Creating a Virtual Environment

Select the virtualization technology to be used; there are a number of quality products, both free and commercial, available to investigators from companies such as VMware, Microsoft, Oracle, and Citrix. When choosing a solution, investigators should be aware that some will require a dedicated host.

Listed below are several considerations when selecting any virtual environment.

1. Support for Operating System Versions (Current)
2. Support for Operating System Versions (Older)
3. Support for Multiple Types of Architectures
4. Support for "Snapshot" Functionality
5. The Solution Contains Protection Mechanisms
6. The Solution has Convenience Features (File Transfers)

Static Analysis

There are two general categories of malware analysis; the first is called "static," and the second is called "dynamic" (which will be addressed later in this domain). Static analysis allows investigators to make a quick assessment of the file. The examination does not execute the code, but basic executable capabilities can still be identified.

Unfortunately, malware code can be quite complex, so static analysis cannot provide the investigator with full program details.

Identifying Malicious Files

One of the first challenges investigators may encounter is assessing the general nature of a file and creating a state that provides useful information. Malware is created in many varieties and the extension does not necessarily determine its purpose. For example, executable files exist with no ".EXE" extension and malware does not have to be an executable file if it relies on an associated "helper" application to activate its functionality.

Malware may also be compressed, packed, or encrypted, making it difficult to identify and analyze. If the malware was detected by antivirus software and quarantined, the malware file will be encoded in a proprietary format which does not allow it to execute on a system. This proprietary encoding also makes it difficult to analyze.

Researching Malware Files

There are a number of known file databases that have created millions of files that other organizations have examined. When initially working with a malware sample, use a cryptographic hash to uniquely identify the file contents. The preferred hashing algorithms are Message-Digest 5 (MD5) and Secure Hash Algorithm 1 and 2 (SHA1 and SHA2).

Investigators should be aware that many knowledge repositories use MD5, not SHA1/2. Use an establishing tool to generate the hash (such as *md5deep*, *WinMD5*, or *DigestIT2004*). Once the hash values of the suspected malware have been computed, the next step is to begin researching accurate information. Listed below are several respected sources of information for researching malware.

1. Bit9's FileAdvisor
2. VirusTotal

3. ThreatExpert

4. National Software Reference Library (NIST)

Researching File Headers

A "file header" is a small number of bytes at the beginning of a file that can help identify what type of file it is. Referred to as a "Magic Number," it is the first 16 bytes in a file that identify the type. Identification tools are available to assist investigators with analysis – such as McAfee's *FileInsight* Hex Editor – simplifying the process of inspecting file headers for patterns.

Portable Executable Files

If a Portable Executable (PE) file is discovered, it must be inspected with a tool specializing in parsing the PE formats and providing additional information. Many varieties of PE files exist, posing significant analysis challenges for investigators. However, becoming aware of those challenges sooner than later will assist teams in their triage process. Challenges include PE files which are "packed" or encrypted, making it difficult to determine what compiler created the binary.

Identifying "Packed" Files

If an executable file contains only a few intelligible strings, or a low number of imports, the file may be "packed." This type of executable file has been subjected to additional process with the intention of compressing and/or obfuscating the code. While the process significantly changes the files' content, it retains all of its functionality.

It is worth doing some quick research on the packer type that the tool detects to see if there is a simple way to handle the file. Some packing tools are open source, making tools to unpack these files readily available. Some PE analysis tools – such as *PE Explorer* – also have the capability to unpack files, although occasionally "debuggers" must be used to assist in the process.

Domain 15: *Static and Dynamic Malware Triage*

Introduction to Dynamic Analysis

During dynamic analysis, a highly controlled monitoring system is put into place and the malware is executed. This type of analysis has limitations and can be extremely challenging. Getting the malware to execute properly in a controlled environment is difficult, and execution does not guarantee the functionality will be fully revealed. However, it can confirm the findings of static analysis and reveal new facts about the malware file itself.

Automated Analysis: Sandboxes

Automated dynamic analysis tools, or "sandboxes," tend to be easy to use and generate a wealth of information. The investigator simply inputs the malware sample and the system generates an analysis report. Public sandboxing options are available – such as GFI Sandboxing – for organizations in which an in-house capability would be cost prohibitive.

However, public sandboxes may not be the best option in some circumstances. There are several reasons listed below for not using a publicly available sandbox when conducting analysis; all these reasons should be considered by investigators.

1. **Client Non-Disclosure Agreements**: In many cases, suspected malware contains sensitive information about the victim organization and related systems. NDA's may prohibit the release of proprietary or sensitive information about the organization to third-parties.

2. **Policy, Contract, and Regulatory**: Contingent upon the industry or location of the organization, laws and policies may prohibit the sharing of sensitive information to third-parties for any reason. The risks and penalties of violating these restrictions are severe and often not worth the costs, as the sandbox solution may not even provide the answers needed to assist in the investigation.

3. **Sandbox Solutions Slow to Evolve**: New versions and families of malware are released daily which require the

managing agencies of the sandbox solutions to continually change their analysis process – a virtually impossible task.

Introduction to Manual Dynamic Analysis

Manual dynamic analysis requires a general understanding of how an operating system loads and executes programs. While this process allows greater flexibility for the investigator, it is also challenging and time consuming. Under the best circumstances, getting malware to execute properly is difficult.

If the investigator does not know the context in which the malware was discovered, proper execution of the malware becomes extremely difficult if not impossible.

Malware Runtime Monitoring

Once the suspected malware has been loaded and executed, the actions it takes must be closely monitored. The investigator must also choose a tool – such as Microsoft's *Process Monitor* - that provides a method to log and filter data that is collected during analysis based on certain and specific criteria.

When properly executed, monitoring will allow the investigator to develop a sense of the malwares' functionality and generate additional investigative leads. Listed below are several common areas of interest to investigators when monitoring malware runtime.

1. Process Creation and Changes
2. File Creation and Changes
3. Registry Key Creation and Changes
4. Creating or Changing Network Activity

[This page intentionally left blank]

DOMAIN 15

Static and Dynamic Malware Triage

The following knowledge assessment questions are presented in true / false, multiple choice, and fill-in-the-blank formats. The correct answers are provided in an Answer Key at the end of this text. These questions may or may not be presented on the actual certification exam.

Domain 15: Knowledge Assessment Questions

The results of malware triage can help generate _____ that can then be used to sweep a larger population of systems.

A. Indicators of Compromise

B. Investigative Leads

C. Firewall Rules

D. Antivirus Quarantines

E. All of the Above

Which of the choices listed below is **not** an industry best practices for malware handling procedures?

A. Use a Virtual Environment for Triage

B. Triage on the Primary Operating System

C. Disable "Convenience" Features

D. Ensure the Virtual Environment is Isolated

E. All of the Above

Manual dynamic malware analysis requires a general understanding of how a(n) _____ loads and executes programs.

A. Operating System

B. Malicious File

C. User Application

D. Server Software

E. All of the Above

Which of the choices listed below is an industry best practices for malware handling procedures?

A. Enable "Preview View" Functionality

B. Avoid Configuration or Process Changes

C. Enable Autorun and Automount Features

D. Prominently Label Transport Media

E. All of the Above

Domain 15: *Static and Dynamic Malware Triage*

There are many reasons not to use a publicly available sandbox when conducting analysis; these include client non-disclosure agreements, policy restrictions, and _____.

A. Contract Restrictions

B. Regulatory Requirements

C. Slow Sandbox Evolution

D. Third-Party Data Leaks

E. All of the Above

Which of the choices listed below is **not** an industry best practices for malware handling procedures?

A. Use a CD with Large Bold Font

B. Store in a Directory that Denies Execution

C. Ensure Handling as Privileged User

D. Password Protected and Encrypted Archive

E. All of the Above

An executable file that has been subjected to additional processes for the purpose of obfuscating the original code is said to be "_____."

A. Compressed

B. Packed

C. Encrypted

D. Corrupted

E. All of the Above

Which of the choices listed below is **not** a characteristic or capability of a virtual malware triage environment?

A. Does not Require Physical Hardware

B. Promotes Resource Contention

C. Configuration is Highly Flexible

D. Eliminates Cross-Contamination

E. All of the Above

Domain 15: *Static and Dynamic Malware Triage*

In general, forensic investigators should not access _____ for many reasons, some of which can affect their organization as well as others.

A. Confidential Information

B. Unrelated Evidence

C. Outside Investigations

D. Malicious Websites

E. All of the Above

Which of the options listed below is **not** one of the eight high-level steps required to perform an effective remediation?

A. Form the Remediation Team

B. Establish Forensic Lab Protocols

C. Determine the Timing of the Remediation

D. Develop Remediation Posturing Actions

E. All of the Above

It is an industry best practice to perform malware triage in appropriate and _____ triage environments.

A. Confidential

B. Expedient

C. Formally Designated

D. Client Site

E. All of the Above

Which of the choices listed below is a valid reason why forensic investigators should avoid any contact with known malicious websites?

A. Actions May "Tip Off" Attackers

B. "Malicious Site" may be a Victim

C. May Disrupt Operations of Good Actors

D. May Unknowingly Break Laws

E. All of the Above

Manual dynamic analysis requires a general understanding of how an operating system loads and executes programs.

1. True

2. False

During dynamic analysis, a highly controlled monitoring system is put into place and the malware is studied without executing the program.

1. True

2. False

If a Portable Executable File (PE) is discovered, it must be inspected with a tool specializing in parsing the PE format and providing additional information.

1. True

2. False

There are two general categories of malware analysis; the first is called "non-secured," and the second is called "actively secured."

1. True

2. False

One of the first challenges an investigator may encounter is assessing the general nature of a file and creating a state that provides useful information.

1. True

2. False

If an executable file contains only a few intelligible strings, or a low number of imports, the file may be discarded as irrelevant to the investigation.

1. True

2. False

DOMAIN 16

Forensic Strategies
for Incident Remediation

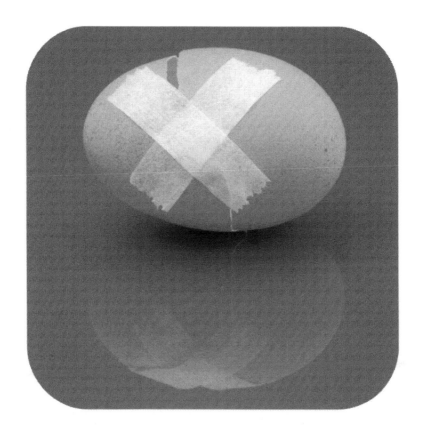

Effective Remediation: Overview

Effective Incident Response requires a two-pronged approach: incident investigation and incident remediation. Remediation of large incidents is a complex endeavor, involving many high-level remediation steps and action types.

There are two primary goals of this phase of Incident Response: remediation of the current incident and improving the overall security posture of the victim organization. Although it may be tempting, making wide, sweeping changes to improve security posture during any remediation is not advisable.

Many actions listed in the remediation plan – which will be revised many times before implementation – will prove to be more difficult than anticipated and be shifted to strategic planning initiatives for future consideration.

Effective Remediation: Planning Approaches

The level of detail will always vary between incidents. Ultimately, the final planning strategy and level of detail included in the plan will be the responsibility of the assigned remediation owner. Some organizations rely on high-level planning with very few details. Other organizations choose to create a detailed plan including Microsoft Project workflows, Excel spreadsheets, and other documents.

Regardless of the approach taken, the Incident Response Team must ensure the remediation plan is comprehensive, implementable, and the individualized assigned to remediation tasks are both respected and trusted.

Effective Remediation: High-Level Steps

There is no single strategy to a successful remediation effort; the right strategy depends on a number of factors specific to the incident. However, listed below are nine high-level steps typically taken during any remediation action.

1. Form the Remediation Team
2. Determine the Timing of the Remediation
3. Develop the Remediation Posturing Actions
4. Develop the Containment Actions
5. Develop the Eradication Plan
6. Determine the Eradication Event Timing
7. Develop the Strategic Recommendations
8. Document the Areas for Improvement
9. Document the Lessons Learned

Effective Remediation: Lessons Learned

Once the "Lessons Learned" documentation has been generated after the remediation of the incident, ensure they are stored in a known central location. These documents should be available to investigators and response personnel as needed but restricted to these personnel only.

Study these documents will help improve the organization over time and increase the probability that future incidents will be handled in an efficient and effective manner.

Effective Remediation: Considerations

Regardless of the incident type, listed below are seven common factors that are typically specific to each incident that must be considered by those who will plan for – and be involved with – any Incident Response actions.

1. Incident Severity
2. Remediation Event Timing
3. Remediation Team Composition
4. Existing and Available Technology
5. Available Budget and Finances
6. Management and Senior Leadership Support
7. Public Scrutiny of the Organizations

Remediation Plan Pre-Checks

This may sound unnecessary, but it is especially important that senior leadership support the overall plan and communicate the decision to declare an incident response. Any Incident Response will consume many hours and require key individuals within the organization be temporarily reassigned for the response.

It is also important to verify a remediation owner has been assigned to provide leadership for stakeholders and ensure the highest probability of an effective and cohesive Incident Response.

Creating the Remediation Team

One goal of the Incident Response Team is to strive for a low "Mean Time to Remediate" (MTTR), which can be accomplished by choosing remediation team members wisely. A low MTTR is critical to the organization as it reduces the elapsed time between incident discovery and eradication. The remediation team is created when the incident investigation is initiated and begins planning the remediation actions immediately.

Assigning a Remediation Owner: General Knowledge

The first and most important consideration when forming the remediation team is assigning an effective remediation owner. The remediation owner accepts responsibility for the overall effort and interacts with both technical and non-technical personnel.

Listed below are non-technical knowledge areas with which the remediation owner should be familiar.

1. Organizational Operations
2. Organizational Strategy
3. Public Relations
4. Human Resources
5. Legal Counsel

Assigning a Remediation Owner: Considerations

A good project manager may be able to lead a remediation effort if they are surrounded by an effective team. However, it is better to select a senior technical person who possesses a high-level of both technical and non-technical skills, as they will be able to provide better direction for the team.

The remediation owner must also have the authority to make decisions and the support of senior leadership to do so. This will facilitate the effective resolution of disagreements and the ability to implement difficult decisions.

Assigning a Remediation Owner: Key Qualities

There are times when a single person has responsibility for the investigation and the remediation, especially with less complex incidents. In larger incidents, the remediation owner will be separate from the investigation owner and the incident owner. In either case, there are five key qualities listed below that every remediation owner candidate should possess.

1. A Thorough Understanding of IT and Security
2. A High Degree of Focus on Execution
3. An Understanding of Internal Politics
4. A Proven Record of Building Support
5. Communications Skills Across all Disciplines

Remediation Team Members

Remediation teams are cross-functional by nature and bring a diverse set of skill sets to the Incident Response. This facilitates valuable insights into attacker activities and an understanding of the feasibility of proposed actions. Regardless of discipline, the team members must possess the authority to make decisions and implement changes as needed.

Direct team members include technical representatives from Investigations, System and Network Management, and DevOps /

Application Management. Ancillary team members represent internal and external legal counsel, business managers, human resources, public relations, and senior leadership.

Timing of the Remediation

There are three primary approaches to any remediation action after an incident: *immediate, delayed,* and *combined.* The typical default timing of an Incident Response is *delayed action.*

1. **Immediate Action**: This type of response is appropriate when the actions of the attacker simply cannot be allowed to continue for any reason – such as the theft of funds or sensitive data – and investigating the incident would cause additional harm by delaying any response.

2. **Delayed Action**: This type of response is appropriate when the actions of the attacker have not yet caused any harm to the organization. This allows investigators to investigate the incident, thoroughly scope the level of compromise, identify any existing malware and attack vectors, plan the eradication and remediation actions, and thoroughly document the event and the lessons learned.

3. **Combined Action**: This type of response is appropriate when the actions of the attacker are serious enough to respond immediately but an adequate response has not yet been developed. Investigators have a limited opportunity to investigate the incident but must defer their efforts once a remediation plan is ready to be implemented.

Remediation Posturing Actions: Purpose

Posturing actions are taken during an ongoing incident and are designed to be implemented with minimum impact on the attacker. These actions can enhance the investigative teams' visibility into the incident and provide additional sources of evidence. Implementing high-level posturing actions early in the incident life cycle may also decrease the time spent in later incident phases.

Domain 16: *Forensic Strategies for Incident Remediation*

Listed below are examples of high-level posturing actions which can be implemented without alerting an attacker.

1. Enhanced Logging   (System-Specific)
2. Enhanced Logging   (Application-Specific)
3. Enhanced Logging   (Network-Specific)

Remediation Posturing Actions: Basic Measures

Many of the actions listed below can be addressed by simply improving the type of data retained by the endpoints, while others serve to enhance the overall security posture of the organization.

1. Centralize Authentication Logs
2. Centralize SIEM Log Files
3. Enhance Event-Based Alerting
4. Patch Third-Party Applications
5. Implement Multifactor Authentication
6. Reduce Critical Data Storage Locations
7. Enhance Native Security Authentication

Remediation Posturing Actions: Enhanced Auditing

The specific audit events that are logged will depend on the scope of the incident, and the goals of the remediation effort. Listed below are several auditing actions typically enhanced during an ongoing incident.

1. Audit Failed Logon Events
2. Audit Successful Logon Events
3. Audit Account Management
4. Audit Object Access
5. Audit Privilege Use
6. Audit Process Tracking
7. Audit System Events

Remediation Posturing Actions: Application Security

A common posturing goal is to increase the security of an application or system without alerting the attacker. Prior to implementing the actions listed below, the investigative teams should be consulted to determine if the actions will cause the attacker to notice changes in the network environment.

1. Remove LANMAN Hashing (Windows)
2. Strengthen Password Security
3. Patch Commonly Targeted Applications
4. Employ Multifactor in Uncompromised Environments
5. Fix Application Flaws Used by the Attacker

Remediation Posturing Actions: Considerations

In some instances, it is acceptable to remove a compromised system from the environment; systems are rebuilt all the time and attackers expect some degree of flux in a network environment. If 25-30 infected systems are taken offline simultaneously, however, an attacker will most likely assume they have been discovered. If this occurs, it can seriously impede the investigation and remediation effort.

Implications of Alerting an Attacker

As stated above, taking actions that alerts an attacker they have been discovered is usually considered detrimental to the investigation. The attacker will most likely react to their discovery. If the attacker is confident presence can be maintained in the environment their response many be benign.

If the attacker is cautious the tools, tactics, and processes (TTP's) used may change, causing investigators to reassess their TTP's as well. If the attacker is cautious, a strategy of dormancy and/or obfuscation may be employed. If the attacker is angry a strategy of offensive and destructive action – such as overwhelming a network with compromised systems – may be employed. When implemented correctly, posturing actions should not alert attackers and cause them to react or respond.

Basic Incident Containment Actions

Containment actions prevent the attacker from performing a specific action that the organization cannot allow to continue. They are typically considered extreme as the attacker will be made aware almost immediately they have been detected. Containment actions will not remove an attackers' access from the network but can prevent further access if implemented properly. Listed below are a few containment actions typically employed during Incident Response.

1. Remove the Attackers' Ability to Authenticate
2. Remove the Attackers' Access to Server Hosting
3. Require Two-Person Integrity Checks
4. Implement Notifications for Critical Areas

Eradication Plan Development: Overview

Eradication actions are implemented during a short period to remove the attacker from the environment. They typically occur when the victim organization has fully recovered and all access by the attacker has been removed. This requires the environment to be fully scoped – including all compromised systems, accounts, and known attack vectors – with the goal of restoring trust in the network.

Eradication Plan Development: Defensive Actions

Eradication plans should be designed with the expectation that the attacker will try to regain access to the environment. Listed below are several defensive actions that serve to deny the attacker further access to the environment.

1. Disconnect the Victim from the Internet (Eradication)
2. Block Known Malicious IP Addresses

   3. Blackhole Relevant Domain Names
   4. Change all User Account Passwords
   5. Implement any Planned Network Segmentation
   6. Mitigate the Original Vulnerabilities
   7. Rebuild the Compromised Systems

Eradication Plan Development: Timing

In most organizations, weekends are a good time to conduct an eradication event because disruption to the operations is minimal. Investigators should take the time to discover the attackers' working hours to maximize the potential success of the eradication effort and to minimize the chance the attacker discovers their lack of access. The timing of the eradication event will be contingent upon the severity of the incident.

Eradication Plan Development: Delayed Response

The longer the duration of the eradication event, the greater the chance that the attacker will regain access to the environment.
In the event regains access to the environment the Incident Response Team will be forced to reinvestigate and attempt to contain the compromise again. This will delay the scheduled eradication event and may start the Incident Response process over from the beginning.

Eradication Plan Development: Changing Passwords

An eradication event action item that is often difficult to implement is changing all user and system passwords. Listed below are several accounts investigators must consider when planning password changes during the plan development.

   1. Windows, Linux, and Mac Accounts
   2. Service Accounts
   3. Local Administrator and Root Accounts
   4. Integrated Credential Database Accounts

5. Application Accounts
6. Networking Device Accounts
7. Database Accounts

Eradication Plan Development: Password Challenges

Changing passwords is challenging enough when things are going well; during an Incident Response, investigators should be prepared to develop contingencies for common complications. Users who are on vacation or traveling for organizational reasons may not be able to change their passwords in a timely manner.

Accounts which are inactive but not disable will have no user available to change the password and administrators must identify these accounts to change the passwords themselves. Systems outside the incident domain – but related and interfaced – may not be compelled to implement password changes.

Eradication Timing and Execution

An ideal time to execute the eradication event is when the team has properly scoped the compromise and implemented posturing actions. The timing of the eradication event is critical. If executed too early the incident may not be fully scoped and the attackers' access not fully removed, causing the eradication to fail.

If executed too late the organization risks the attacker changing TTP's or accomplishing the mission. The ideal timing for an eradication is referred to as the "strike zone."

Eradication Timing and Execution: The "Strike Zone"

Determining when you are in the "strike zone" can be difficult; it's more of an art than a science. The following conditions listed below are good indicators the time is right to execute the eradication plan.

1. Good Visibility into the Breached Area

2. Good Understanding of the Attackers' TTP's
3. Daily Compromises Decrease Significantly
4. The Remaining Compromises are Known IOC's
5. The Remediation Effort is Thoroughly Planned

Eradication Timing and Execution: Planning

The planning process for the eradication event should start as soon as the incident owner has decided upon a remediation approach. The plan will always be considered a "work in progress" as it is frequently updated based on new information.

Early planning contributes to effective remediation, and agreement between owners – incident, investigation, and remediation – is important.

Once all owners agree, do not let the eradication date slip away or get continually pushed back. Doing so makes difficult implementations nearly impossible to execute.

Eradication Timing and Execution: System Remediation

Once the networking actions have been completed, the system and application administrators can start remediating compromised systems. Verification is needed to ensure the systems are properly rebuilt and effective communication throughout this process is critical.

Some administrators will attempt to clean a system instead of rebuilding it; this is not advised as trace malware could still reside on systems after they have been cleaned. Listed below are a few reasons the verification process is important for every system in the network.

1. Systems may be Accidentally Overlooked
2. Systems may be Improperly Rebuilt
3. Rebuilding of Systems may Never Occur

Develop Strategic Recommendations

Strategic recommendations are actions deemed critical to the organizations' security posture but cannot be implemented during the eradication. They are often developed during the course of the first two phases of the remediation.

Strategic recommendations are typically difficult to implement and disruptive in nature but offer significant enhancements to an organizations' security posture.

Good suggestions may be offered as part of the remediation effort – such as a comprehensive restructuring of the network architecture – but are not feasible in the short-term due to time, planning, and resource constraints. In these cases it makes sense to shift these suggestions forward and include them when considering post-incident strategic recommendations.

Document Lessons Learned

Create lessons learned for any remediation effort that requires significant participation, planning, and implementation. They should be created as soon as possible to ensure information is accurately captured.

Investigators may have trouble remembering specific information as time passes and compiling information from key personnel who have returned to their full-time assignments may be difficult.

Consider making this documentation an official and mandatory part of the remediation effort; this tends to encourage the taking of notes during an incident.

Additionally, creating a lessons learned document will greatly reduce the time and effort necessary to plan another enterprise-wide password change in the event that becomes necessary.

Listed below are several best practices that will serve to assist investigators when creating post-incident lessons learned documentation.

1. **Use Document Templates**: Templates ensure a degree of structure and standardization during investigative reporting and serves to facilitate a consistency in the process as well.

2. **Make Documents Accessible**: Store the lessons learned documentation in a centralized location, making them accessible to Incident Response Team members with a "need to know." Wikis and document management systems are typical storage solutions for this type of documentation.

3. **Make Documents Searchable**: Documents should be easily searchable and browsable for reference purposes. Consider the use of tags, categories, and keywords to facilitate this process. In addition to their value as effective training tools, easily searchable documents tend to prevent duplicate lessons learned documentation from being created.

[This page intentionally left blank]

DOMAIN 16

Forensic Strategies
for Incident Remediation

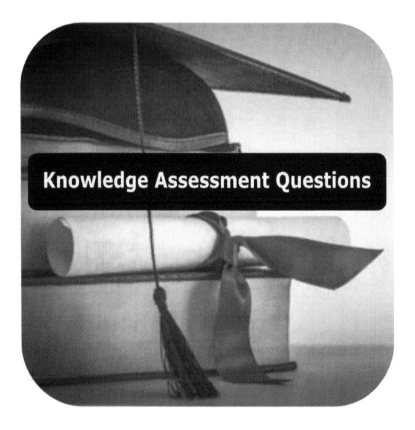

Knowledge Assessment Questions

The following knowledge assessment questions are presented in true / false, multiple choice, and fill-in-the-blank formats. The correct answers are provided in an Answer Key at the end of this text. These questions may or may not be presented on the actual certification exam.

Domain 16: Knowledge Assessment Questions

An understanding of _____ is one of the five key characteristics to look for when assigning a remediation owner to develop a team

A. Internal Politics

B. Global Issues

C. Management Theory

D. Social Media

E. All of the Above

Which of the options listed below is **not** one of the seven common factors specific to incidents that must be considered when engaged in Incident Response?

A. Level of Incident Severity

B. Composition of the Remediation Team

C. Existing and Available Technology

D. Location of the Victim Organization

E. All of the Above

When assigning a remediation owner to develop a team, it is best to choose a _____ to ensure the highest possibility of a successful outcome.

A. Member of Management

B. Senior Technical Person

C. Senior Project Manager

D. Third-Party Provider

E. All of the Above

Which of the options listed below is **not** one of the three primary approaches to any remediation action after an incident?

A. Delayed

B. Structured

C. Combined

D. Immediate

E. All of the Above

Domain 16: *Forensic Strategies for Incident Remediation*

The remediation owner assigned to an Incident Response Team must have an understanding and working knowledge of _____ to ensure the highest possibility of a successful outcome.

A. Available Technology

B. Organizational Strategy

C. Public Relations Strategy

D. Human Resource Strategy

E. All of the Above

Which of the options listed below will **not** enhance the investigative teams' visibility and add additional sources of evidence when implementing remediation posturing actions?

A. Increase Biometric Security

B. Remove Systems from the Network

C. Restrict Remote Network Access

D. Develop Geofencing Procedures

E. All of the Above

Effective remediation planning includes documenting _____ that should be stored in a secure centralized environment.

A. Security Procedures

B. Business Responsibilities

C. Third-Party Actions

D. Areas of Improvement

E. All of the Above

Which of the options listed below is **not** a good indicator that the Incident Response Team is in the "strike zone" and ready for an eradication event?

A. Understanding of Attackers' TTP's

B. Daily Compromises Decrease Greatly

C. Remediation Effort is Thoroughly Planned

D. Limited Visibility into the Breached Area

E. All of the Above

Domain 16: *Forensic Strategies for Incident Remediation*

The _____ must be complete prior to an eradication event and will probably be revised many times.

A. Remediation Steps

B. Incident Response Plan

C. Draft Remediation Plan

D. Action Types

E. All of the Above

Which of the options listed below is **not** a good strategic recommendation that can be offered after an incident to increase an organizations' security posture?

A. Implement Strict Network Segmentation

B. Remove User Privileges

C. Upgrade to More a Secure O/S

D. Implement Egress Traffic Filtering

E. All of the Above

The remediation owner will form and develop the remediation team when the _____ have been officially approved and initiated.

A. Incident Investigative Actions

B. Incident Posturing Actions

C. Incident Containment Actions

D. Incident Eradication Actions

E. All of the Above

Which of the options listed below is **not** a basic incident containment action that can be implemented by an Incident Response Team?

A. Remove the Attackers' Ability to Authenticate

B. Discontinue Notifications in Critical Areas

C. Require Two-Person Integrity Checks

D. Remove Access to Server Hosting

E. All of the Above

Domain 16: *Forensic Strategies for Incident Remediation*

Effective incident response requires a two-pronged approach: incident containment, and incident eradication.

1. True
2. False

The remediation owner accepts responsibility for the overall effort and interacts with both technical and non-technical personnel.

1. True
2. False

Posturing actions are taken during an ongoing incident and are designed to be implemented with maximum impact on the attacker.

1. True
2. False

The strategic recommendations are often developed during the course of the first two phases of the remediation.

1. True
2. False

The longer the duration of the eradication event, the less likely the chance that the attacker will regain access to the environment.

1. True
2. False

Eradication plans should be designed with the expectation that the attacker will try to regain access to the environment.

1. True
2. False

Certified Network Forensic Analysis Manager

Knowledge Assessment
ANSWER KEY

Domain 01: Knowledge Assessment Answer Key

Incident Response is a _____ and structured approach to go from incident detection to resolution.

C. Coordinated

Incident Response is a coordinated and structured approach to go from incident detection to resolution.

Which of the following characteristics is **not** a discipline of network forensic investigations?

D. Internal Time Considerations

Internal time considerations does not represent the discipline of network forensics. External threats dictate the response timeline.

The first stage in the seven stages of the Attack Life Cycle Model is _____.

B. Initial Compromise

The first stage in the seven stages of the Attack Life Cycle Model is the Initial Compromise.

Which of the following statements does **not** apply to the Initial Compromise phase of the Attack Life Cycle Model?

C. Install a Persistent Backdoor

The installation of a persistent backdoor occurs during the Maintain a Foothold phase of the Attack Life Cycle Model.

When an attacker first attempts to compromise a victim's system, one of the least likely methods to be employed with be to _____.

C. Access a Server Console

When an attacker first attempts to compromise a victim's system, one of the least likely methods to be employed with be to access a server console.

Which of the following statements applies to the Escalate Privileges phase of the Attack Life Cycle Model?

E. All of the Above

All of the choices presented apply to the Escalate Privilege phase of the Attack Life Cycle Model.

When an attacker conducts internal reconnaissance within a compromised network, the goal of that effort is to _____ .

E. All of the Above

All of the choice presented represent actions an attacker would take to conduct internal reconnaissance of a network.

Which of the following statements does **not** apply to the Internal Reconnaissance phase of the Attack Life Cycle Model?

A. Workflow Reporting

An attacker would analyze information flows during the Internal Reconnaissance phase of the Attack Life Cycle Model. Workflow reporting is a function of the business process.

The second stage in the seven stages of the Attack Life Cycle Model is _____.

A. Establish a Foothold

The second stage in the seven stages of the Attack Life Cycle Model is to establish a foothold.

Which of the following statements applies to the Establish Foothold phase of the Attack Life Cycle Model?

B. Establish C2 with the Victim System

An attacker will gain command and control over a victims' system in the Establish Foothold phase of the Attack Life Cycle Model.

Definition of Incident: "*Any unlawful, _____, or unacceptable action that involves a computer system, cell phone, tablet, and any other electronic device with an operating system, or that operates in a computer network.*"
C. Unauthorized

Definition of Incident: "*Any unlawful, unauthorized, or unacceptable action that involves a computer system, cell phone, tablet, and any other electronic device with an operating system, or that operates in a computer network.*"

The seventh step taken by an investigator conducting an Incident Response is _____.
B. Document Lessons Learned

The seventh step taken by an investigator conducting an Incident Response is to document lessons learned.

Incident Response is an informal and flexible approach to go from incident detection to resolution.
2. **False**

Incident Response is a coordinated and structured approach to go from incident detection to incident resolution.

Digital forensics focuses on independent devices and is primarily preemptive, while network forensics focuses on networked devices and is primarily reactive.
2. **False**

Digital forensics focuses on independent devices and is primarily reactive, while network forensics focuses on networked devices and is primarily dynamic and preemptive.

In the discipline of network forensics, internal time considerations drive and shape the investigators' live acquisition strategies.

2. **False**

In the discipline of network forensics, external time considerations drive and shape the investigators' live acquisition strategies.

The field of digital forensics typically has a moderate dependency on log files, while network forensics typically relies on a critical dependency on log files.

1. **True**

The field of digital forensics typically has a moderate dependency on log files, while network forensics typically relies on a critical dependency on log files.

Not all seven stages are always part of the attack life cycle, but this model can be adapted to fit any incident.

1. **True**

Not all seven stages are always part of the attack life cycle, but this model can be adapted to fit any incident.

The discipline of Network Forensics focuses on data at rest on post-mortem images located on independent devices.

2. **False**

The discipline of Network Forensics focuses on data in motion on live systems located on networked devices.

Domain 02: Knowledge Assessment Answer Key

_____ will typically only allow data packets which pass specific security criteria (rules) to enter or leave a network or a segment of a network.
A. Firewalls

Firewalls will typically only allow data packets which pass specific security criteria (rules) to enter or leave a network or a segment of a network.

Which of the choices listed below is considered to be an advantage of a Unified Threat Management device?
D. Avoids Redundancy of Capabilities

Avoiding a redundancy of capabilities is considered to be an advantage of a Unified Threat Management device.

A _____ may look like a traditional hardware firewall but is an efficient security tool that combines multiple systems into a single platform.
B. UTM Device

A UTM device may look like a traditional hardware firewall but is an efficient security tool that combines multiple systems into a single platform.

Which of the choices listed below is considered to be a characteristic or function of a firewall?
C. Operates on a Rule-Based Configuration

Operating on a rule-based configuration is considered to be a characteristic or function of a firewall.

A _____ uses configured rules to monitor the state of network connections such as TCP streams, UDP datagrams, and ICMP messages.
C. Stateful Firewall

A stateful firewall uses configured rules to monitor the state of network connections such as TCP streams, UDP datagrams, and ICMP messages.

Which of the choices listed below is considered to be a characteristic or function of an Intrusion Protection System (IPS)?

B. Evaluates Anomalous Behaviors of Threats

The evaluation of anomalous behaviors and threats is considered to be a characteristic or function of an Intrusion Protection System (IPS).

A _____ inspects a data packets' destination address, calculates the best way for it to reach its destination, and then forwards it accordingly.

D. Network Router

A network router inspects a data packets' destination address, calculates the best way for it to reach its destination, and then forwards it accordingly.

Which of the choices listed below is considered to be a characteristic or function of stateful firewall inspection?

A. Inspects Individual Packets in Isolation

The inspection of individual packets in isolation is considered to be a characteristic or function of stateful firewall inspection.

A(n) _____ is a piece of software running on a single host that can restrict incoming and outgoing network activity for that host only.

A. Host-Based Firewall

A host-based firewall is a piece of software running on a single host that can restrict incoming and outgoing network activity for that host only.

Which of the choices listed below is a report an investigator would expect to find when reviewing IDS / IPS log information?

D. Errors on Network Devices

Errors on network devices is a report an investigator would expect to find when reviewing IDS / IPS log information.

A(n) _____ provides rules that are applied to port numbers or IP addresses, each with hosts and/or networks permitted to use the service.

B. Access Control List

An access control list provides rules that are applied to port numbers or IP addresses, each with hosts and/or networks permitted to use the service.

Which of the choices listed below is considered to be a characteristic or function of an unmanaged network switch?

C. Allows Communication without Collisions

Allowing communications without collisions is considered to be a characteristic or function of an unmanaged network switch.

A router is a security monitoring device that controls incoming and outgoing network traffic based on predetermined security rules.

2. **False**

A firewall is a security monitoring device that controls incoming and outgoing network traffic based on predetermined security rules.

As robust as UTM's sound and as important a role as they play in providing security to networks, there are several weaknesses that can be exploited.

1. **True**

As robust as UTM's sound and as important a role as they play in providing security to networks, there are several weaknesses that can be exploited.

Network switches use input from the data source, destination address, and other key values to assess whether network traffic will be allowed.
2. **False**

Stateless firewalls use input from the data source, destination address, and other key values to assess whether network traffic will be allowed.

An Intrusion Prevention System is a security / threat prevention technology that analyzes network traffic and takes automated actions when needed.
1. **True**

An Intrusion Prevention System is a security / threat prevention technology that analyzes network traffic and takes automated actions when needed.

A host-based firewall is a device that connects other network devices and manages the flow of data by directing and sending packets to the intended recipient.
2. **False**

A network switch is a device that connects other network devices and manages the flow of data by directing and sending packets to the intended recipient.

An access control list provides rules that are applied to port numbers or IP addresses, each with hosts and/or networks permitted to use the service.
1. **True**

An access control list provides rules that are applied to port numbers or IP addresses, each with hosts and/or networks permitted to use the service.

Domain 03: Knowledge Assessment Answer Key

Most enterprises utilize _____ to assign IP addresses to devices connected to the network.
B. Dynamic Host Configuration Protocol

Most enterprises utilize Dynamic Host Configuration Protocol to assign IP addresses to devices connected to the network.

Which of the statements listed below is **not** an example of the functionality of the LANDesk Software Management Suite?
C. Records are Purged when the Application is Deleted

The functionality of the LANDesk Software Management Suite can maintain records even when the application is deleted.

Logging is enabled by default on _____, and a number of fields have been added to log files over time.
C. Microsoft Servers

Logging is enabled by default on Microsoft servers, and a number of fields have been added to log files over time.

Which McAfee log file in the list provided below provides the forensic investigator with the most useful and relevant information during Incident Response actions?
C. OnAccessScanLog.txt

McAfee's *OnAccesScanLog.txt* log file can provide the most useful and relevant information during Incident Response actions.

An issue for forensic investigators to be aware of is that the "date" and "time" fields in Microsoft Dynamic Host Configuration Protocol logs are generated in _____ time.
D. Local Time

An issue for forensic investigators to be aware of is that the "date" and "time" fields in Microsoft Dynamic Host Configuration Protocol logs are generated in local time.

Which of the statements listed below is an example of the functionality and characteristics of standard Web Servers?
D. Configurable for Virtual Host Capability

Common functionality and characteristics of standard Web servers includes the capability of configuring virtual hosts.

There are three primary sources of evidence derived from database server log files available to forensic investigators: Client Connection Logs, User Query Logs, and _____.
A. System Error Logs

There are three primary sources of evidence derived from database server log files available to forensic investigators: Client Connection Logs, User Query Logs, and system error logs.

Which of the statements listed below is **not** an example of the functionality of Trend Micro Office Scan Antivirus Suite?
A. Stores Evidence Centrally on Domain Controllers

The Trend Micro Office Scan Antivirus Suite's functionality does not include storing evidence centrally on domain controllers.

Symantec quarantine files are stored in a proprietary format with a .VBN extension and includes the file metadata and _____.
A. Encoded Original

Symantec quarantine files are stored in a proprietary format with a .VBN extension and includes the file metadata and an encoded original.

Which of the statements listed below is **not** an example of the functionality of a Domain Name System (DNS) server?

B. Assign Device MAC Addresses

The assigning of MAC addresses is not a functionality of Domain Name System (DNS) servers.

Web servers are typically configured to utilize Port 80 for HTTP traffic and Port _____ for HTTPS traffic (Secure Socket Layer).

C. 443

Web servers are typically configured to utilize Port 80 for HTTP traffic and Port 443 for HTTPS traffic (Secure Socket Layer).

Which Database Server log file in the list provided below provides the forensic investigator with the most useful and relevant information during Incident Response actions?

E. All of the Above

All of the choices presented provide the forensic investigator with useful and relevant information during Incident Response actions.

The most important aspect of DHCP is the assignment of IP addresses to systems, called a DHCP lease.

1. **True**

The most important aspect of DHCP is the assignment of IP addresses to systems, called a DHCP lease.

An issue to be aware of is that the "date" and "time" fields in Microsoft DHCP logs are generated in the Coordinated Universal Time (UTC) format that is difficult to understand.

2. **False**

An issue to be aware of is that the "date" and "time" fields in Microsoft DHCP logs are generated in local time.

The Domain Name System (DNS) is a system that stores information primarily about host names.

1. **True**

The Domain Name System (DNS) is a system that stores information primarily about host names.

In many instances, the antivirus product will log an error (because it cannot read an encrypted file) that includes the file size and type of malware family from which it is derived.

2. **False**

In many instances, the antivirus product will log an error (because it cannot read an encrypted file) that includes a file name and path.

McAfee provides a threat intelligence portal where analysts can obtain more detailed information about threats detected by VirusScan.

1. **True**

McAfee provides a threat intelligence portal where analysts can obtain more detailed information about threats detected by VirusScan.

Web servers receive and respond to requests from clients, such as web browsers, using the File Transfer Protocol (FTP).

2. **False**

Web servers receive and respond to requests from clients, such as web browsers, using the Hypertext Transfer Protocol (HTTP).

Domain 04: Knowledge Assessment Answer Key

Which choice below is a characteristic of *The Open Group Architecture Framework* that provides an approach for developing enterprise architecture?

D. Defines the System Components

The defining of system components is a characteristic of *The Open Group Architecture Framework* that provides an approach for developing enterprise architecture.

Modern networks and usage patterns no longer resemble those that made traditional _____ a practical solution years ago.

A. Perimeter Defense

Modern networks and usage patterns no longer resemble those that made traditional perimeter defense a practical solution years ago.

Select the best choice below for the following definition: *"An enterprise ontology that provides a fundamental and formalized structure for enterprise architecture."*

C. Zachman Framework

The Zachman Framework is an enterprise ontology that provides a fundamental and formalized structure for enterprise architecture.

The _____ identifies and defines the organizations' strategy, governance, structure, goals, and key business processes.

B. Business Architecture

The business architecture identifies and defines the organizations' strategy, governance, structure, goals, and key business processes.

Which choice below is a potential risk and/or attack vector associated with Zero Trust Networks that can undermine its utility?

B. Control Plane Security

Control plane security is a potential risk and/or attack vector associated with Zero Trust Networks that can undermine its utility.

_____ is/are complex technological components of security architecture that are crucial for the protection of information assets.

C. Cryptographic Services

Cryptographic services are complex technological components of security architecture that are crucial for the protection of information assets.

Select the best choice below for the following definition: "*Describes the hardware, software, and network infrastructure needed to support the deployment of a solution.*"

A. Technology Architecture

The technology architecture describes the hardware, software, and network infrastructure needed to support the deployment of a solution.

The _____ is where most vulnerabilities are presented and the greatest effort in reducing vulnerabilities is expended.

D. Application Layer

The Application layer is where most vulnerabilities are presented and the greatest effort in reducing vulnerabilities is expended.

Which choice below is one of the six phases comprising the Software Development Life Cycle (SDLC)?

D. Planning

Planning is one of the six phases comprising the Software Development Life Cycle (SDLC).

A(n) _____ is a document which provides recommended integrations of products and services to form a solution.

A. Reference Security Architecture

A Reference Security Architecture is a document which provides recommended integrations of products and services to form a solution.

Select the best choice below for the following definition: *"Complex technological components of security architecture that are crucial for the protection of information assets."*

C. Cryptographic Services

Cryptographic services are complex technological components of security architecture that are crucial for the protection of information assets.

The _____ documents solution deployments, system interactions, and their relationships to core business processes.

D. Application Architecture

The application architecture documents solution deployments, system interactions, and their relationships to core business processes.

The TOGAF Framework is an enterprise ontology that provides a fundamental and formalized structure for enterprise architecture.

2. **False**

The Zachman Framework is an enterprise ontology that provides a fundamental and formalized structure for enterprise architecture.

The granularity of data stored within a trust agent can vary based on the needs of the organization and maturity of the system.

1. **True**

The granularity of data stored within a trust agent can vary based on the needs of the organization and maturity of the system.

Border protection is typically thought of as the component technological devices that provide security at the transport layer.

2. **False**

Border protection is typically thought of as the component technological devices that provide security at the network layer.

Technology architecture describes the hardware, software, and network infrastructure needed to support the deployment of a solution.

1. **True**

Technology architecture describes the hardware, software, and network infrastructure needed to support the deployment of a solution.

Identity management is implemented to ensure that a solution remains in the configuration for which is was originally intended.

2. **False**

Configuration management is implemented to ensure that a solution remains in the configuration for which is was originally intended.

The perimeter model attempts to build a wall between trusted and untrusted sources; zero trust assumes all actors are malicious.

1. **True**

The perimeter model attempts to build a wall between trusted and untrusted sources; zero trust assumes all actors are malicious.

Domain 05: Knowledge Assessment Answer Key

The actions taken by a forensic network investigator when performing any kind of data analysis include _____.
E. All of the Above

All of the choices presented are actions that would be taken by a forensic network investigator performing any kind of data analysis.

Which of the following options should forensic investigators **not** consider as a goal when responding to a network incident?
D. Identification of all Malware

Forensic investigators should not consider the identification of all malware a goal when responding to a network incident.

Most of the challenges a forensic network investigator may face when responding to an Incident Response are _____.
A. Non-Technical

Most of the challenges a forensic network investigator may face when responding to an Incident Response are non-technical.

Which of the following representatives from the victim organization should be considered for participation on the Incident Response Team?
E. All of the Above

All of the choices presented should considered for participation on the Incident Response Tea.

The forensic investigator should view _____ as potential incidents until and investigation proves otherwise.
C. Suspicious Events

The forensic investigator should view suspicious events as potential incidents until and investigation proves otherwise.

When developing an Incident Response Team capability within a victim organization, which of the following options should **not** be considered by a forensic investigator?

B. Scope of the Incident

The scope of an incident is determined when the incident occurs, not in the planning stages of an Incident Response Team.

Forensic investigators should consider contracting external resources through _____ so that communications are reasonably protected from disclosure.

D. Legal Counsel

Forensic investigators should consider contracting external resources through legal counsel so that communications are reasonably protected from disclosure.

When vetting the soft skills of potential members of the Incident Response Team, which of the following should **not** be considered as a prerequisite for acceptance?

A. History of Promotion

History of promotion is not a prerequisite when vetting potential members for an Incident Response Team.

During traditional investigations not involving _____, the forensic examination analysis portion of the investigation consumes the most time.

C. Intrusion

During traditional investigations not involving intrusion, the forensic examination analysis portion of the investigation consumes the most time.

When planning the initial response interview activities, who should the forensic investigator include in the first round of interviews to be conducted?

E. All of the Above

All the choices presented should be included in the first round of interviews conducted by the forensic investigator.

Live response analysis is a critical part of the Incident Response process when network investigators observe suspicious activity but have limited _____.

A. Details

Live response analysis is a critical part of the Incident Response process when network investigators observe suspicious activity but have limited details.

Which of the following is **not** a reason for a forensic investigator to pursue a memory collection strategy during live acquisition?

C. Answer High-Level Questions

Answering high-level questions is not a reason for investigators to pursue a memory collection strategy during live acquisition.

The core principles of investigating a computer security incident are inherently different from a non-technical investigation.

2. **False**

The core principles of investigating a computer security incident are identical to those used in non-technical investigations.

Indicators of Compromise (IOC) creation is the process of documenting the characteristics and the artifacts of an incident in a structured manner.

1. **True**

Indicators of Compromise (IOC) creation is the process of documenting the characteristics and the artifacts of an incident in a structured manner.

Acting on incomplete and/or inaccurate information is acceptable if a reasoned response based on factual data may take more time to investigate.

2. **False**

Acting on incomplete and/or inaccurate information is never acceptable if a reasoned response based on factual data may take more time to investigate.

Snort rules help Incident Response investigators by differentiating between normal internet activities and malicious activities in real time.

1. **True**

Snort rules help Incident Response investigators by differentiating between normal internet activities and malicious activities in real time.

Prioritization during an Indicator of Compromise (IOC) investigation is based solely on the criticality of data and/or the critical business process affected by the compromise.

2. **False**

Prioritization during an Indicator of Compromise (IOC) investigation is based on many factors in addition to the criticality of data and/or the critical business process affected by the compromise.

When responding to incidents in which intrusion is not suspected, disk imaging is a standard operating procedure.

1. **True**

When responding to incidents in which intrusion is not suspected, disk imaging is a standard operating procedure.

Domain 06: Knowledge Assessment Answer Key

Which choice below refers to any influence that changes, obscures, adds, contaminates, or obliterates evidence regardless of intent?
A. Evidence Dynamics

Evidence dynamics refers to any influence that changes, obscures, adds, contaminates, or obliterates evidence regardless of intent.

_____ define(s) the elements of a claim and are typically driven by the primary consumer of the investigative report.
C. Elements of Proof

Elements of proof define the elements of a claim and are typically driven by the primary consumer of the investigative report.

Which choice below is the first action an Incident Response Team investigator should take when documenting any interview?
C. Prepare a List of Interview Questions

Preparing a list of interview questions is the first action an Incident Response Team investigator should take when documenting any interview.

The non-verbal cue referred to as _____ can be defined as, "*A pattern in which the sender gives conflicting messages on verbal and nonverbal levels.*"
B. Incongruent Communication

The non-verbal cue referred to as incongruent communication can be defined as, "*A pattern in which the sender gives conflicting messages on verbal and nonverbal levels.*"

Which choice below refers to the documentation of acquisition, control, analysis, and disposition of physical and digital evidence?
B. Chain of Custody

Chain of custody is the documentation of acquisition, control, analysis, and disposition of physical and digital evidence.

A(n) _____ is a systematic inquiry and/or examination, typically conducted for the purpose of identifying and/or verifying facts.

D. Investigation

An investigation is a systematic inquiry and/or examination, typically conducted for the purpose of identifying and/or verifying facts.

Which choice below is the first action an Incident Response Team investigator should take when managing an incident scene?

D. Approach and Secure the Incident Scene

The first action an Incident Response Team investigator should take when managing an incident scene is approaching and securing the incident scene.

_____ states, "*When a person or object comes into contact with another person or object, a cross-transfer of materials occurs.*"

A. Locard's Principle of Exchange

Locard's Principle of Exchange states, "*When a person or object comes into contact with another person or object, a cross-transfer of materials occurs.*"

What choice below is the primary purpose and importance of evidence dynamics in incident response investigations?

C. Reconstruction of the Incident

The primary purpose and importance of evidence dynamics in incident response investigations is to reconstruct the incident.

Regardless of the type of investigation being conducted—physical or digital—_____ items should be a part of the investigative toolkit.

C. Standard

Regardless of the type of investigation being conducted—physical or digital—standard items should be a part of the investigative toolkit.

What choice below is **not** a best practice for investigators when conducting and documenting any type of interview?

B. Ask "Yes" and "No" Questions

Asking "yes" or "no" questions does not represent a best practice for investigators when conducting and documenting any type of interview.

The non-verbal cue referred to as _____ can be defined as, *"The non-lexical component of communication such as intonation, pitch and speed of speaking."*

A. Paralanguage

The non-verbal cue referred to as paralanguage can be defined as, *"The non-lexical component of communication such as intonation, pitch and speed of speaking."*

All case types and investigations have the same considerations—whether the goal is litigation or developing a stronger security posture.

2. **False**

Every case type and investigation has its own considerations—whether the goal is litigation or developing a stronger security posture.

Regardless of the type of investigation being conducted—physical or digital—standard items should be a part of the investigative toolkit.

1. **True**

Regardless of the type of investigation being conducted—physical or digital—standard items should be a part of the investigative toolkit.

Evidence Dynamics refers to any influence that changes, obscures, adds, contaminates, or obliterates networks or systems regardless of intent.

2. **False**

Evidence Dynamics refers to any influence that changes, obscures, adds, contaminates, or obliterates evidence regardless of intent.

In most investigations, interviews are the primary tool investigators use to find out what happened and/or verify physical and technical evidence.

1. **True**

In most investigations, interviews are the primary tool investigators use to find out what happened and/or verify physical and technical evidence.

We respond to thousands of verbal cues and behaviors including postures, facial expression, eye gaze, gestures, and tone of voice.

2. **False**

We respond to thousands of nonverbal cues and behaviors including postures, facial expression, eye gaze, gestures, and tone of voice.

Preparation is the key to so many endeavors in life and interviewing potential targets and witnesses during investigations is no exception.

1. **True**

Preparation is the key to so many endeavors in life and interviewing potential targets and witnesses during investigations is no exception.

Domain 07: Knowledge Assessment Answer Key

When formatting an Incident Response report, forensic investigators can benefit by utilizing formal reporting guidelines, language guidelines, and _____.
C. Standard Templates

When formatting an Incident Response report, forensic investigators can benefit by utilizing formal reporting guidelines, language guidelines, and standard templates.

Which best practice for external communication should a forensic investigator utilize when involved in any type of incident response?
E. All of the Above

All of the choices presented represent best practices for a forensic investigator to utilize when involved in any incident response.

When defining the Incident Response mission, the ability to _____ is not a critical goal of the forensic investigator.
D. Allocate Financial Resources

When defining the Incident Response mission, the ability to allocate financial resources is not a critical goal of the forensic investigator.

Defining the Incident Response mission in advance will keep the team focused and set realistic goals. Which consideration below does **not** support this initiative?
C. Purchase External Hard Drives

The purchase of external hard drives does not support defining the Incident Response mission and setting realistic goals.

Forensic investigators should place a high level of importance on _____ when selecting the tools needed for Incident Response in field environments.
A. Portability

Forensic investigators should place a high level of importance on portability when selecting the tools needed for Incident Response in field environments.

Daubert v. Merrell (1993) shifted focus from a test for general acceptance to a test for reliability and relevance. Which answer below does **not** apply to the case?
D. Is the Technique Successful in Court?

Daubert v. Merrell (1993) did not address the question, "*Is the technique successful?*" when it shifted focus from a test for general acceptance to a test for reliability and relevance

In preparation for conducting network forensics in a field environment, investigators should maintain a set of _____ interfaces in their response toolkits.
E. All of the Above

All of the choices presented are interfaces an investigator should maintain in their response toolkits.

When conducting an Asset Management Survey, which of the following should be documented by the Incident Response Team?
B. Date the Device was Provisioned

The date the device was provisioned should be documented by the Incident Response Team during an Asset Management Survey.

Forensic investigators involved with Incident Response must plan to take _____ into consideration when preparing to assess computing device configuration on a network infrastructure.
E. All of the Above

All of the choices presented are elements that should be taken into consideration when preparing to assess computing device configuration on a network infrastructure.

When conducting an Asset Management Survey, which of the following should **not** be documented by the Incident Response Team?

A. IOC Creation and Search Utilities

IOC creation and search utilities should not be considered by the Incident Response Team during an Asset Management Survey.

An organizations' _____, software inventories, and other documentation will rarely provide a forensic investigator with the entire IT infrastructure picture.

C. Standard System Build

An organizations' standard system build, software inventories, and other documentation will rarely provide a forensic investigator with the entire IT infrastructure picture.

When conducting a Network Resource Survey, which of the following should be documented by the Incident Response Team?

D. IT Management Software

IT Management software should be documented by the Incident Response Team when conducting a Network Resource Survey.

The majority of incidents involving networks will require investigators to perform forensic work outside of a lab environment.

1. **True**

The majority of incidents involving networks will require investigators to perform forensic work outside of a lab environment.

Use approved and established channels for external communications, such as Business Unit managers or Human Resource personnel, to avoid unintentional disclosures.

2. **False**

Use approved and established channels for external communications, such as Public Relations managers or Legal Counsel personnel, to avoid unintentional disclosures.

Kumbo Tire Co et al. v. Carmichael et al (1993) shifted the focus from a test for general acceptance to a test for reliability and relevance.

2. **False**

Kumbo Tire Co et al. v. Carmichael et al (1993) shifted the focus from a test for reliability and relevance to scientific methodology.

There is no strict definition for "forensically sound": a judge will decide the admissibility of evidence on a case-by-case basis.

1. **True**

There is no strict definition for "forensically sound": a judge will decide the admissibility of evidence on a case-by-case basis.

Good human resource practices and sound business management policies promote rapid response and enhance the remediation process.

2. **False**

Good information security practices and change management policies promote rapid response and enhance the remediation process.

When considering network resource logs, examine each process and service within the environment to better understand where logging is retained and how it is controlled.

1. **True**

When considering network resource logs, examine each process and service within the environment to better understand where logging is retained and how it is controlled.

Domain 08: Knowledge Assessment Answer Key

From a general forensic analysis standpoint, various categories of data evidence may be available to an investigator which may include Windows Registry, Unix Syslog, and _____.
E. All of the Above

All of the choices presented are categories of data evidence that are available to investigators for forensic analysis.

Which of the questions listed below is **not** relevant for defining the objectives to be used when performing analysis?
C. What Team Members will Participate?

Knowing which team members will participate is not relevant for defining the objectives to be used when performing analysis.

Once a forensic investigator has obtained data to analyze, one of the first challenges they may encounter is determining how to _____ it.
D. Access

Once a forensic investigator has obtained data to analyze, one of the first challenges they may encounter is determining how to access it.

Which of the choices listed below is **not** one of the four high-level categories of data sources available to the network investigator?
A. BYOD Smart Phones and Tablets

BYOD smart phones and tablets are not considered to be one of the four high-level categories of data sources for investigators.

An investigator can search systems for artifacts of data manipulation or theft, and these artifacts can reveal an attackers' _____.
C. Methodology

An investigator can search systems for artifacts of data manipulation or theft, and these artifacts can reveal an attackers' methodology.

Which of the choices listed below is **not** a preferred external resource that can be utilized by network investigators during Incident Response actions?
B. Bulletin Board Systems and/or Social Media

Bulletin Board Systems and social media are not preferred external resources that can be utilized by network investigators during Incident Response actions.

_____ analysis is typically used in cases in which an investigator does not know exactly what they are looking for or how the information can be found.
A. Statistical

Statistical analysis is typically used in cases in which investigators do not know exactly what they are looking for or how the information can be found.

Which of the choices listed below is **not** one of the characteristics and capabilities of the analysis technique referred to as "file carving"?
C. Can be Affected by File Extensions

The characteristics and capabilities of the "file carving" technique during analysis are not affected by file extensions.

When evaluating results during the analysis process, it is important for investigators to identify potential _____ early in the process to avoid misleading conclusions.
D. False Positives or Negatives

When evaluating results during the analysis process, it is important for investigators to identify potential false positives and/or negatives early in the process to avoid misleading conclusions.

Which of the choices listed below is an example of information sought by forensic investigators when conducting network analysis?

E. All of the Above

All of the choices presented represent and action or characteristic associated with evaluating collected data.

When evaluating and prioritizing analytical results, it is important to consider the _____ to ensure accurate answers to investigative questions.

B. Relevant Investigative Context

When evaluating and prioritizing analytical results, it is important to consider the relevant investigative context to ensure accurate answers to investigative questions.

Which of the choices listed below accurately represents the information sought by forensic investigators when conducting network analysis?

E. All of the Above

All of the choices presented accurately represents the information sought by investigators when conducting network analysis.

Investigative questions and information may provide leads, but keep in mind they could be partially or completely false.

1. **True**

Investigative questions and information may provide leads, but keep in mind they could be partially or completely false.

You can search systems for artifacts of data manipulation or theft, although these artifacts will not reveal an attackers' methodology.

2. **False**

You can search systems for artifacts of data manipulation or theft, and these artifacts can reveal an attackers' methodology.

Several analysis methods are commonly used across many different types of operating systems, disk images, log files, and other data.
1. **True**

Several analysis methods are commonly used across many different types of operating systems, disk images, log files, and other data.

When engaged in "file carving," the idea is to search for a common sequence of bytes that corresponds to the body (the first few bytes) of a file.
2. **False**

When engaged in "file carving," the idea is to search for a unique sequence of bytes that corresponds to the header (the first few bytes) of a file.

The "string" or "keyword" search is a basic analysis method that digital investigators have used since the creation of computer forensics.
1. **True**

The "string" or "keyword" search is a basic analysis method that digital investigators have used since the creation of computer forensics.

Most structured data, meaning data with a parsable record format, is well suited for sorting and filtering.
2. **True**

Most structured data, meaning data with a parsable record format, is well suited for sorting and filtering.

Domain 09: Knowledge Assessment Answer Key

Event-based monitoring relies on indicators (or _____) matched against traffic observed by the network sensor.

B. Signatures

Event-based monitoring relies on indicators (or signatures) matched against traffic observed by the network sensor.

Which of the options listed below is **not** a viable outcome when making the case for network monitoring?

D. Identify all Parties Involved

Identifying all parties involved does not represent a viable outcome when making the case for network monitoring.

Statistical monitoring focuses on the high-level view of what _____, or connections, are traversing the network.

D. Information Flows

Statistical monitoring focuses on the high-level view of what information flows, or connections, are traversing the network.

Which of the statements listed below is **not** a characteristic or capability of event-based alerting in network environments?

C. Any Network Event Triggers Alerts

Only events programmed by the network administrator represent the characteristics and capabilities of event-based alerting in network environments.

Intrusion Detection System platforms cannot reliably perform both intrusion detection and _____ duties simultaneously.

B. Network Surveillance

Intrusion Detection System platforms cannot reliably perform both intrusion detection and surveillance duties simultaneously.

Which of the statements listed below is **not** a condition in which network investigators would utilize statistical monitoring?
B. Complete Visibility of the Endpoints

A complete visibility of endpoints does not represent a condition in which network investigators would use statistical monitoring.

Poorly written signatures can cause the network monitoring software to drop packets simply because they _____ cannot keep up with the data flow.
D. Signature Engine

Poorly written signatures can cause the network monitoring software to drop packets simply because the signature engine cannot keep up with the data flow.

Which of the questions listed below accurately represent considerations of forensic investigators planning a network sensor deployment?
E. All of the Above

All of the choice presented represent considerations of forensic investigators planning a network sensor deployment.

In some situations, data captured by a(n) _____ or network device is the only evidence that actions were taken by an attacker.
C. Network Sensor

In some situations, data captured by a network sensor or network device is the only evidence that actions were taken by an attacker.

Which of the steps listed below is not an action for implementing and maintaining a network surveillance program?

C. Consider Platform Security when Feasible

Considering platform security does not accurately represent the required actions for implementing and maintaining a network surveillance program.

The configuration and security of the network sensor are relevant to the potential _____ it may capture.

C. Evidence

The configuration and security of the network sensor are relevant to the potential evidence it may capture.

Which statement listed below is **not** a potential network logging challenge encountered by forensic investigators attempting to gather and analyze data?

B. Log Data is Stored in Similar Formats

Log data stored in similar formats is not a potential network logging challenge encountered by investigators attempting to gather and analyze data.

Event-based monitoring relies on indicators (or signatures) matched against traffic observed by the network sensor.

1. **True**

Event-based monitoring relies on indicators (or signatures) matched against traffic observed by the network sensor.

Statistical monitoring focuses on the low-level view of what network devices, such as Intrusion Detection Systems (IDS), are located on the network.

2. **False**

Statistical monitoring focuses on the high-level view of what information flows, or connections, are traversing the network.

The means by which the header and packet capture is performed is also affected by the purposes of the investigation.
1. **True**

The means by which the header and packet capture is performed is also affected by the purposes of the investigation.

Firewalls only allow system administrators an extensive amount of high-level data flow information when creating audit logs.
2. **False**

Firewalls allow system administrators an extensive amount of granularity when creating audit logs.

Poorly written signatures can cause the software to drop packets simply because the signature engine cannot keep up with the data flow.
1. **True**

Poorly written signatures can cause the software to drop packets simply because the signature engine cannot keep up with the data flow.

Host-based sensors cannot detect the alteration of a system library, or the addition of files in sensitive locations.
2. **False**

Host-based sensors may detect the alteration of a system library, or the addition of files in sensitive locations.

Domain 10: Knowledge Assessment Answer Key

The _____ checklist is not one of the standard forms used by forensic investigators when collecting initial facts during network incidents.

B. Vendor Details

The vendor details checklist is not one of the standard forms used by forensic investigators when collecting initial facts during network incidents.

What standardized measure of time are network investigators most likely to use during Incident Response missions?

B. Coordinated Universal Time

Coordinated Universal Time (UTC) is the standardized measure of time most likely to be used during Incident Response missions.

When completing an Incident Summary Checklist, the _____ is a critical piece of information for the forensic investigator.

D. Category of the Incident

When completing an Incident Summary Checklist, the category of incident is a critical piece of information for the investigator.

When forensic investigators are collecting initial facts during a network incident, which of the following surveys should **not** be utilized by the Incident Response Team?

A. IT Personnel Checklist

An IT Personnel Checklist should not be used by the Incident Response team to collect initial facts regarding network incidents.

When completing an Incident Detection Checklist, the _____ is a critical piece of information for the forensic investigator.

C. Contributing Data Source

Domain 10: *Initiating Network Forensic Investigations*

When completing an Incident Detection Checklist, the contributing data source is a critical piece of information for the investigator.

When completing an Incident Summary Checklist, which of the following should **not** be documented by the network investigator?
D. Updates to Network Configurations

Investigators should document updates to network configurations when completing a Network Details Checklist.

When completing a System Details Checklist, the _____ is a critical piece of information for the forensic investigator.
A. IT Asset Tag Number

When completing a System Details Checklist, the IT asset tag number is a critical piece of information for the investigator.

When completing an Incident Detection Checklist, which of the following should **not** be documented by the network investigator?
A. Remediation Steps Already Taken

Investigators should document remediation steps already taken when completing a System Details Checklist.

When completing a Network Details Checklist, the _____ is a critical piece of information for the forensic investigator.
C. Remediation Steps Taken

When completing a Network Details Checklist, the remediation steps already taken is a critical piece of information for the forensic investigator.

When completing a System Details Checklist, which of the following should **not** be documented by the network investigator?
C. External Malicious IP Addresses

Investigators should document external malicious IP addresses taken when completing a Malware Details Checklist.

When completing a Malware Details Checklist, the following are critical pieces of information for the forensic investigator accept
_____.
B. Personnel Aware of the Incident

When completing a Malware Details Checklist, the following are critical pieces of information for the forensic investigator accept the personnel aware of the incident.

When completing a Network Details Checklist, which of the following should be documented by the network investigator?
B. Process Used to Preserve Data

The process used to preserve data should be documented by the forensic investigator on the Network Details Checklist.

Documenting details about the network is important, even in cases where network details do not seem initially important.
1. **True**

Documenting details about the network is important, even in cases where network details do not seem initially important.

Investigators should follow the practice of grouping systems into single documents; consolidating system details makes it easy to reference required information and answer specific, relevant questions.
2. **False**

Investigators should avoid grouping systems into single documents; it is easy to overlook details and miss specific, relevant questions.

When completing the Malware Details Checklist, the goal of this stage of the investigation is to assemble the facts and circumstances surrounding the discovery of the incident.

1. **True**

When completing the Malware Details Checklist, the goal of this stage of the investigation is to assemble the facts and circumstances surrounding the discovery of the incident.

It is important for investigators to realize that events must be entered in chronological order (when they happened, not when they were discovered).

2. **False**

It is important for investigators to realize that events typically will not be entered in chronological order (when they discovered, not when they were happened).

The Incident Summary Checklist is utilized to gather additional details about how incident was detected and the detection system themselves.

2. **False**

The Incident Detection Checklist is utilized to gather additional details about how incident was detected and the detection system themselves.

A large number of answers to the points in the Malware Detection Checklist are not likely to be answered until much later in the investigation (if at all).

1. **True**

A large number of answers to the points in the Malware Detection Checklist are not likely to be answered until much later in the investigation (if at all).

Domain 11: Knowledge Assessment Answer Key

An example of a _____-based indicator would be a cryptographic hash that could be cross-references against known hashes in a resource library.

D. Property

An example of a property-based indicator would be a cryptographic hash that could be cross-references against known hashes in a resource library.

Which of the following statements would **not** apply to a network investigator attempting to define leads of value?

D. The Lead must be True

Investigators cannot determine a lead is true until the investigation confirms and validates its truth.

Forensic investigators should be aware that _____ when considering reporting a network incident to law enforcement.

E. None of the Above

None of the choices presented should influence the decision to report a network incident to law enforcement.

When a network investigator is conducting interviews and resolving internal leads, which of the actions listed below is a best practice that should be followed?

A. Allow the Interviewee to Tell a Story

Allowing an interviewee to tell their story is a best practice that should be followed when conducting initial interviews.

The final step taken by forensic investigators in the Life Cycle of Indicator Generation is to _____.

A. Publish Indicators

Domain 11: *Initial Development of Leads*

The final step taken by forensic investigators in the Life Cycle of Indicator Generation is to publish the indicators.

What statement listed below is **not** a valid reason for a network investigator to seek out the assistance and involvement of law enforcement during an Incident Response?

C. Civil Cases Help Criminal Cases

A consideration when seeking the assistance of law enforcement is that successful criminal cases (prosecution) helps civil cases.

When resolving internal lead, forensic investigators should _____ to lessen the possibility of biased and misleading information.

D. Avoid Leading Questions

When resolving internal lead, forensic investigators should avoid leading questions to lessen the possibility of biased and misleading information.

What statement listed below is a valid reason for a network investigator to seek out the assistance and involvement of law enforcement during an Incident Response?

E. All of the Above

All of the choices presented are valid reasons for an investigator to seek the assistance and involvement of law enforcement.

An example of a _____-based indicator would be a portable executable file that creates an anomaly in a network information flow.

B. Methodology

An example of a methodology-based indicator would be a portable executable file that creates an anomaly in a network information flow.

Domain 11: *Initial Development of Leads*

Which of the following statements would apply to a network investigator attempting to define leads of value?
A. Determine the Leads' Context

Determining the leads' context would apply to a network investigator attempting to define leads of value.

It is important for forensic investigators to ensure that the properties of a new indicator do not identify the malware or activity _____ at a specific point in the lifecycle.
D. Solely

It is important for forensic investigators to ensure that the properties of a new indicator do not identify the malware or activity solely at a specific point in the lifecycle.

Which of the choices listed below is a methodology-based indicator of interest to an investigator responding to a network incident?
B. Unexpected Executable File

An unexpected executable file would represent a methodology-based indicator of interest to an investigator responding to an incident.

Sorting the good leads from the bad is important, especially when the organization has a fully staffed team with ample time to conduct the investigation.
2. **False**

Sorting the good leads from the bad is important, especially when the organization has a limited team with limited time.

Indicator generation is an iterative process with a goal of generating robust, sustainable signatures to generate reliable information.
1. **True**

Indicator generation is an iterative process with a goal of generating robust, sustainable signatures to generate reliable information.

Leads can result in either host-based indicators or network-based indicators, but never a combination of both.

2. **False**

Leads can result in either host-based indicators or network-based indicators, or a combination of both.

The key items for investigator case notes are personnel involved and the scope of the incident; automated processes will help streamline this situation.

2. **False**

The key items for investigator case notes are actions taken and dates they occurred; no automated process will help in this situation.

Investigators must ensure the indicator verification process identifies data relevant to the indicator and how the data changes over time in the indicator itself.

1. **True**

Investigators must ensure the indicator verification process identifies data relevant to the indicator and how the data changes over time in the indicator itself.

The primary justification for avoiding notification is to avoid losing control of an investigation to law enforcement; additionally, notification of criminal acts is rarely required.

2. **False**

The primary justification for avoiding notification is simply to avoid a public relations issue; notification of criminal acts is rarely required.

Domain 12: Knowledge Assessment Answer Key

One of the serious challenges faced by the forensic investigator when performing a live response is that the action could crash the system in question or _____.

A. Delete Evidence

One of the serious challenges faced by the forensic investigator when performing a live response is that the action could crash the system in question or deletion of evidence.

There are serious potential challenges to performing a live response. Which of the questions listed below would **not** apply to a network investigator considering a live response?

B. Has Verbal Approval been Received?

A network investigator considering a live response must receive written approval to proceed with the acquisition.

Throughout an investigation, forensic investigators must continuously evaluate what data to collect based on how quickly and effectively _____.

D. Questions are Answered

Throughout an investigation, forensic investigators must continuously evaluate what data to collect based on how quickly and effectively questions are answered.

Which of the questions listed below would **not** apply to a network investigator considering the selection of a live response tool?

A. Have the Results been Successful in Court?

An investigator would not consider whether results using the tool have been successful in court when selecting it for live response.

Domain 12: *Principles of Live Data Collection*

Some live response data is inherent to the specific operating system, and some live response data comes from common sources such as _____.

D. Log Files

Some live response data is inherent to the specific operating system, and some live response data comes from common sources such as log files.

Which of the options listed below represents common live response data available to the network investigator?

E. All of the Above

All the choices presented above represents common live response data available to the network investigator

Most forensic toolkits will successfully deal with UAC (User Access Control) but _____ may still be required to access a system.

B. "Run as Administrator"

Most forensic toolkits will successfully deal with UAC (User Access Control) but "Run as Administrator" may still be required to access a system.

Which of the following choices listed below represents a challenge to an investigator attempting to perform a live response?

B. Cannot Connect Removable Media

The inability to connect removable media to a system represents a challenge when attempting to perform a live response.

Forensic network investigators are required to secure _____ before conducting any type of live response acquisition.

C. Written Approval

Domain 12: *Principles of Live Data Collection*

Forensic network investigators are required to secure written approval before conducting any type of live response acquisition.

Which of the statements listed below is **not** a best practice for an investigator engaged in the live response?
C. Fully Automate the Collection Process

Relying solely on a fully automated collection practice does not represent a best practice when engaged in a live response.

As techniques in live response and forensics evolve, _____ and procedures must be continually evaluated.
A. Available Tools

As techniques in live response and forensics evolve, available tools and procedures must be continually evaluated.

Which of the choices listed below can greatly affect the available evidence, leaving some questions unanswered?
B. Operating System Settings

Operating system settings can greatly affect the available evidence and leave some questions unanswered.

Compared to digital forensics, there is a significantly lower potential for challenges when conducting a live response during a network forensic investigation.
2. **False**

Compared to digital forensics, there is a significantly higher potential for challenges when conducting a live response during a network forensic investigation.

Throughout an investigation, investigators continuously evaluate what data to collect based on how quickly and effectively questions are answered.
1. **True**

Domain 12: *Principles of Live Data Collection*

Throughout an investigation, investigators continuously evaluate what data to collect based on how quickly and effectively questions are answered.

It is important to note that operating system settings minimally affect the available evidence, allowing investigators to answer all questions required to produce leads.

2. **False**

It is important to note that Operating system settings can greatly affect the available evidence and leave questions unanswered.

Most forensic toolkits will deal with UAC (User Access Control), but the "Run as Administrator" may still be required.

1. **True**

Most forensic toolkits will deal with UAC (User Access Control), but the "Run as Administrator" may still be required.

As an industry best practice, make every effort to collect data in the order in which it is discovered and take all measures to protect non-volatile data wherever possible.

2. **False**

As an industry best practice, make every effort to collect data in the order of volatility and take all measures to protect volatile data wherever possible.

Do not use the suspect system to perform analysis; this can make the discernment of attacker activity from responder activity difficult.

1. **True**

Do not use the suspect system to perform analysis; this can make the discernment of attacker activity from responder activity difficult.

Domain 13: Knowledge Assessment Answer Key

Each NTFS volume will contain its own _____ stored within the volume root as a file named "$MFT."

D. Master File Table

Each NTFS volume will contain its own Master File Table stored within the volume root as a file named "$MFT."

Which choice listed below describes a function or characteristic of Volume Shadow Copies (VSC)?

A. Automated Processes Trigger Snapshots

The automated process of triggering snapshots of a users' system describes a function of Volume Shadow Copies (VSC).

The benefit of _____ entries (including slack) is they contain the same metadata as a FileName attribute in the Master File Table.

A. INDX Attribute

The benefit of INDX attribute entries (including slack) is they contain the same metadata as a FileName attribute in the Master File Table.

Which choice listed below describes a function or characteristic of the Resident Data attribute?

B. Contains File Data when Assembled

A function and characteristic of the Resident Data attribute is that is contains file data when assembled.

_____ provide a mechanism for maintaining point-in-time copies of files on an entire volume (aka, "snapshots" and "restore points").

D. Volume Shadow Copies

Volume Shadow Copies (VSC) provide a mechanism for maintaining point-in-time copies of files on an entire volume (aka, "snapshots" and "restore points").

Which choice listed below describes a function or characteristic of the Prefetch performance optimization mechanism?
D. Limited to 128 Entries

A limit of 128 entries is a characteristic of the Prefetch performance optimization mechanism.

All versions of Windows systems maintain three categories of "core" event logs: "_____," "System," and "Security."
D. Application

All versions of Windows systems maintain three categories of "core" event logs: "Application," "System," and "Security."

Which choice listed below describes a characteristic of an event logged in the Windows Security Event log generated by the process tracking function?
B. Full Path to the Executable on the Disk

An event logged in the Windows Security Event log generated by the process tracking function provides a full path to the executable on the disk.

The Windows _____ provides the ability to automatically execute programs at a specific date and time (or recurring).
B. Task Scheduler

The Windows Task Scheduler provides the ability to automatically execute programs at a specific date and time (or recurring).

Which choice listed below describes a characteristic of potential evidence that can be found in the Windows Registry?
A. Significant Insight into User Activity

Potential evidence that can be found in the Windows Registry may yield significant insight into user activity on the system.

_____ refers to a broad range and category of registry keys, file paths, and other components that load and run executable code.

A. Persistence Mechanisms

Persistence mechanisms refers to a broad range and category of registry keys, file paths, and other components that load and run executable code.

Which choice listed below describes a function or characteristic of System Configuration Registry Keys?

D. Network, User, and Security Settings

Network, user, and security settings is a characteristic of System Configuration Registry Keys.

NTFS (NT File System) defines how space is allocated and utilized, how files are created and deleted, and how metadata is stored and updated.

1. **True**

NTFS (NT File System) defines how space is allocated and utilized, how files are created and deleted, and how metadata is stored and updated.

File timestamps (MACE) are among the most important metadata stored in the temporary Recycle Bin for forensic investigators.

2. **False**

File timestamps (MACE) are among the most important metadata stored in the Master File Table for forensic investigators.

The benefit of INDX attribute entries (including slack) is they contain the same metadata as a FileName attribute in the Master File Table.

1. **True**

The benefit of INDX attribute entries (including slack) is they contain the same metadata as a FileName attribute in the Master File Table.

Volume shadow copies are a performance optimization mechanism Microsoft introduced to reduce boot and application loading times.

2. **False**

Prefetch is a performance optimization mechanism Microsoft introduced to reduce boot and application loading times.

The Registry serves as the primary database of configuration data for the Windows operating system and applications that run on it.

1. **True**

The Registry serves as the primary database of configuration data for the Windows operating system and applications that run on it.

By examining the correct Security Control Reinforcement Keys, you can recover everything from the system O/S installation date to current firewall policies and user groups.

2. **False**

By examining the correct System Configuration Registry Keys, you can recover everything from the system O/S installation date to current firewall policies and user groups.

Domain 14: Knowledge Assessment Answer Key

While examining forensic evidence, it is common to find artifacts that are not part of – or dependent upon – the _____.

D. Operating System

While examining forensic evidence, it is common to find artifacts that are not part of – or dependent upon – the operating system.

What choice listed below describes a function or characteristic likely to be encountered by forensic investigators when investigating web browsers?

D. Creates Many System Artifacts

Forensic investigators are likely to discover many system artifacts when investigating web browsers.

If an application is not _____, perform research to determine what artifacts may be useful and where they may be located.

B. Well-Documented

If an application is not well-documented, perform research to determine what artifacts may be useful and where they may be located.

What choice listed below describes an area of interest to forensic investigators when investigating the Google Chrome web browser?

C. Autofill (Enabled by Default)

Autofill (enabled by default) is an area of interest to forensic investigators when investigating the Google Chrome web browser.

_____ are applications that retrieve, process, and present data, and are currently the most popular computer applications in mainstream use.

D. Web Browsers

Domain 14: *Investigating Applications*

Web browsers are applications that retrieve, process, and present data, and are currently the most popular computer applications in mainstream use.

What choice listed below describes a function or characteristic associated with Mozilla's web browser Firefox?

B. Configurable Settings to Clear History

Mozilla's web browser Firefox provides users with configurable settings to clear history.

_____ is a web browser maintained by Microsoft, mostly supported in larger enterprises, and installed by default on the MS O/S.

C. Internet Explorer

Internet Explorer is a web browser maintained by Microsoft, mostly supported in larger enterprises, and installed by default on the MS

What choice listed below describes a function or characteristic associated with Microsoft Outlook for Windows?

A. POP, IMAP, MX, and HTTP-Based

POP, IMAP, MX, and HTTP-Based capabilities is a characteristic associated with Microsoft Outlook for Windows.

_____ was launched in 2008, and steadily grown in popularity to become number one of the top three most widely used web browsers.

B. Google Chrome

Google Chrome was launched in 2008, and steadily grown in popularity to become number one of the top three most widely used web browsers.

What choice listed below describes a function or characteristic associated with the Facebook Chat application?
C. Challenging without Account Access

The Facebook Chat application can be challenging to investigate without account access.

_____ clients provide a way for individuals to have the ability to communicate with each other in (near) real time.
C. Instant Message

Instant Message clients provide a way for individuals to have the ability to communicate with each other in (near) real time.

What choice listed below describes a function or characteristic associated with the Facebook's Messenger application?
B. Allows Communication with "Friends List"

A function associated with the Facebook's Messenger application is the ability users to communicate with others on a "Friends List."

While examining forensic evidence, it is uncommon to find artifacts that are not part of – or dependent upon – the operating system.
2. **False**

While examining forensic evidence, it is common to find artifacts that are not part of – or dependent upon – the operating system.

Before expending effort, check if your preferred forensic suite supports processing the application data that is relevant to the investigation.
1. **True**

Before expending effort, check if your preferred forensic suite supports processing the application data that is relevant to the investigation.

Apple's Safari was launched in 2008, and steadily grown in popularity to become number one of the top three most widely used web browsers.

2. **False**

Google Chrome was launched in 2008, and steadily grown in popularity to become number one of the top three most widely used web browsers.

Surveys indicate that web and mobile-based e-mail now account for more than 50% of all e-mail clients.

1. **True**

Surveys indicate that web and mobile-based e-mail now account for more than 50% of all e-mail clients.

Facebook Chat messages in memory are formatted in Extensible Markup Language (XML), a text format that is not human readable.

2. **False**

Facebook chat messages in memory are formatted in JavaScript Object Notation (JSON), a human-readable text format.

A tool that can parse Facebook Chat messages, along with many other evidence items, is Internet Evidence Finder (IEF).

1. **True**

A tool that can parse Facebook chat messages, along with many other evidence items, is Internet Evidence Finder (IEF).

Domain 15: Knowledge Assessment Answer Key

The results of malware triage can help generate _____ that can then be used to sweep a larger population of systems.

A. Indicators of Compromise

The results of malware triage can help generate Indicators of Compromise that can then be used to sweep a larger population of systems.

Which of the choices listed below is **not** an industry best practices for malware handling procedures?

B. Triage on the Primary Operating System

Conducting triage on a primary Operating System is not considered to be a best practice for malware handling procedures.

Manual dynamic malware analysis requires an understanding of how a(n) _____ loads and executes programs.

A. Operating System

Manual dynamic malware analysis requires an understanding of how an Operating System loads and executes programs.

Which of the choices listed below accurately represents an industry best practices for malware handling procedures?

D. Prominently Label Transport Media

Prominently labeling transport media represents an industry best practices for malware handling procedures.

There are many reasons not to use a publicly available sandbox when conducting analysis; these include client non-disclosure agreements, policy restrictions, and _____.

E. All of the Above

All of the choices presented are reasons not to use a publicly available sandbox when conducting analysis.

Which of the choices listed below is **not** an industry best practices for malware handling procedures?
C. Ensure Handling as a Privileged User

Handling malware as a non-privileged user is considered to be an industry best practice for malware handling procedures.

An executable file that has been subjected to additional processes for the purpose of obfuscating the original code is said to be "_____."
B. Packed

An executable file that has been subjected to additional processes for the purpose of obfuscating the original code is said to be "packed."

Which of the choices listed below is not a characteristic or capability of a virtual malware triage environment?
B. Promotes Resource Contention

One of the beneficial characteristics of a virtual malware triage environment is that it does not promote resource contention.

In general, forensic investigators should not access _____ for many reasons, some of which can affect their organization as well as others.
D. Malicious Websites

In general, forensic investigators should not access malicious websites for many reasons, some of which can affect their organization as well as others.

Which of the options listed below is **not** one of the eight high-level steps required to perform an effective remediation?

B. Establish Forensic Lab Protocols

Establishing forensic lab protocols is not considered to be one of the eight high-level steps required to perform an effective remediation.

It is an industry best practice to perform malware triage in appropriate and _____ triage environments.

C. Formally Designated

It is an industry best practice to perform malware triage in appropriate and formally designated triage environments.

Which of the choices listed below is a valid reason why forensic investigators should avoid any contact with known malicious websites?

E. All of the Above

All of the choices presented are valid reasons why forensic investigators should avoid any contact with known malicious websites.

Manual dynamic analysis requires a general understanding of how an operating system loads and executes programs.

1. **True**

Manual dynamic analysis requires a general understanding of how an operating system loads and executes programs.

During dynamic analysis, a highly controlled monitoring system is put into place and the malware is studied without executing the program.

2. **False**

During dynamic analysis, a highly controlled monitoring system is put into place and the malware is executed.

If a Portable Executable File (PE) is discovered, it must be inspected with a tool specializing in parsing the PE format and providing additional information.
1. **True**

If a Portable Executable File (PE) is discovered, it must be inspected with a tool specializing in parsing the PE format and providing additional information.

There are two general categories of malware analysis; the first is called "non-secured," and the second is called "actively secured."
2. **False**

There are two general categories of malware analysis; the first is called "static," and the second is called "dynamic."

One of the first challenges an investigator may encounter is assessing the general nature of a file and creating a state that provides useful information.
1. **True**

One of the first challenges an investigator may encounter is assessing the general nature of a file and creating a state that provides useful information.

If an executable file contains only a few intelligible strings, or a low number of imports, the file may be discarded as irrelevant to the investigation.
2. **False**

If an executable file contains only a few intelligible strings, or a low number of imports, the file may be "packed."

Domain 16: Knowledge Assessment Answer Key

An understanding of _____ is one of the five key characteristics to look for when assigning a remediation owner to develop a team.

A. Internal Politics

An understanding of internal politics is one of the five key characteristics to look for when assigning a remediation owner to develop a team.

Which of the options listed below is **not** one of the seven common factors specific to incidents that must be considered when engaged in Incident Response?

D. Location of the Victim Organization

The location of the victim organization will always be unique and cannot be included as one of the seven common factors specific to Incident Response.

When assigning a remediation owner to develop a team, it is best to choose a _____ to ensure the highest possibility of a successful outcome.

B. Senior Technical Person

When assigning a remediation owner to develop a team, it is best to choose a senior technical person to ensure the highest possibility of a successful outcome.

Which of the options listed below is **not** one of the three primary approaches to any remediation action after an incident?

B. Structured

Immediate, delayed, and combined actions are the three primary approaches to any remediation action after an incident occurs.

The remediation owner assigned to an Incident Response Team must have an understanding and working knowledge of _____ to ensure the highest possibility of a successful outcome.

E. All of the Above

All of the choices presented are disciplines with which the remediation owner must have understanding and knowledge to ensure the highest probability of a successful outcome.

Which of the options listed below will not enhance the investigative teams' visibility and add additional sources of evidence when implementing remediation posturing actions?

E. All of the Above

None of the choices presented are examples of posturing actions that are designed to increase visibility and additional sources of evidence without altering a malicious actor in the network.

Effective remediation planning includes documenting _____ that should be stored in a secure centralized environment.

D. Areas of Improvement

Effective remediation planning includes documenting areas of improvement that are stored in a secure centralized environment.

Which of the options listed below is **not** a good indicator that the Incident Response Team is in the "strike zone" and ready for an eradication event?

D. Limited Visibility into the Breached Area

An Incident Response Team with limited visibility into the breached area will never be able to identify the "strike zone" and know when the eradication event should proceed.

The _____ must be completed prior to an eradication event and will probably be revised many times.
B. Incident Response Plan

The Incident Response Plan must be completed prior to an eradication event and will probably be revised many times.

Which of the options listed below is **not** a good strategic recommendation that can be offered after an incident to increase an organizations' security posture?
B. Remove User Privileges

Removing user privileges denies the network to everyone and is not consider a best practice anywhere, for any reason.

The remediation owner will form and develop the remediation team when the _____ have been officially approved and initiated.
A. Incident Investigative Actions

The remediation owner will form and develop the remediation team when the incident investigative actions have been officially approved and initiated.

Which of the options listed below does not represent a basic incident containment action that can be implemented by an Incident Response Team?
B. Discontinue Notifications in Critical Areas

Effective and continual communication with critical areas is crucial in any incident containment action implemented by the Incident Response Team.

Effective incident response requires a two-pronged approach: incident containment and incident eradication.
2. **False**

Effective incident response requires a two-pronged approach: incident investigation and incident remediation.

The remediation owner accepts responsibility for the overall effort and interacts with both technical and non-technical personnel.
1. **True**

The remediation owner accepts responsibility for the overall effort and interacts with both technical and non-technical personnel.

Posturing actions are taken during an ongoing incident and are designed to be implemented with maximum impact on the attacker.
2. **False**

Posturing actions are taken during an ongoing incident and are designed to be implemented with minimum impact on the attacker.

The strategic recommendations are often developed during the course of the first two phases of the remediation.
1. **True**

The strategic recommendations are often developed during the course of the first two phases of the remediation.

The longer the duration of the eradication event, the less likely the chance that the attacker will regain access to the environment.
2. **False**

The longer the duration of the eradication event, the more likely the chance that the attacker will regain access to the environment.

Eradication plans should be designed with the expectation that the attacker will try to regain access to the environment.
1. **True**

Eradication plans should be designed with the expectation that the attacker will try to regain access to the environment.

C)NFAM Certification Exam Voucher

To purchase your C)NFAM certification exam voucher visit:

phase2advantage.com/exam-vouchers

Phase2 Advantage provides certification exam vouchers to academic and corporate partners responsible for teaching our cybersecurity course content to students, educators, and industry professionals.

DEMONSTRATE MARKETABLE SKILLS

INCREASE CAREER OPPORTUNITIES

CONVENIENT ONLINE TESTING

Vouchers are also available for individuals who need to renew their existing certification or retake an exam to obtain certification. All certification exam vouchers include a **10% discount code**.

C)NFAM Certification Exam Voucher

To purchase your C)NFAM certification exam voucher visit:

phase2advantage.com/exam-vouchers

Phase2 Advantage provides certification exam vouchers to academic and corporate partners responsible for teaching our cybersecurity course content to students, educators, and industry professionals.

DEMONSTRATE MARKETABLE SKILLS

INCREASE CAREER OPPORTUNITIES

CONVENIENT ONLINE TESTING

Vouchers are also available for individuals who need to renew their existing certification or retake an exam to obtain certification. All certification exam vouchers include a **10% discount code**.

Made in the USA
Columbia, SC
22 November 2020